Manage

Your

Time

2nd Edition

By
Ron Fry

CAREER PRESS
180 Fifth Avenue
P.O. Box 34
Hawthorne, NJ 07507
1-800-CAREER-1
201-427-0229 (outside U.S.)
FAX: 201-427-2037

MANAGE YOUR TIME (2ND ED.)

ISBN 1-56414-078-4, $6.95

Cover design by A Good Thing, Inc.

Printed in the U.S.A. by Book-mart Press

To order this title by mail, please include price as noted above, $2.50
handling per order, and $1.00 for each book ordered. Send to: Career
Press, Inc., 180 Fifth Ave., P.O. Box 34, Hawthorne, NJ 07507.

Or call toll-free 1-800-CAREER-1 (Canada: 201-427-0229) to order
using VISA or MasterCard, or for further information on books from
Career Press.

Library of Congress Cataloging-in-Publication Data

Fry, Ronald W.
    Manage your time / by Ron Fry. -- 2nd ed.
        p. cm.
    Includes index.
    ISBN 1-56414-078-4 : $6.95
    1. College students--Time management.   I. Title.
LB2395.4.F79   1994
378.1'7--dc20   94-5492
                                                              CIP

Ron Fry's

HOW TO STUDY
PROGRAM

How to Study, 3rd Ed. (ISBN 1-56414-075-X, 224 pp., $9.95)

"Ace" Any Test, 2nd Ed. (ISBN 1-56414-079-2, 128 pp., $6.95)

Improve Your Memory, 2nd Ed. (ISBN 1-56414-080-6, 128 pp., $6.95)

Improve Your Reading, 2nd Ed. (ISBN 1-56414-077-6, 128 pp., $6.95)

Manage Your Time, 2nd Ed. (ISBN 1-56414-078-4, 128 pp., $6.95)

Take Notes, 2nd Ed. (ISBN 1-56414-076-8, 128 pp., $6.95)

Write Papers, 2nd Ed. (ISBN 1-56414-081-4, 128 pp., $6.95)

Available individually at your favorite bookstore or as a set by calling 1-800-CAREER-1.

STUDY SMARTER, NOT HARDER!

Ron Fry's **HOW TO STUDY** *Program,* the best-selling and most acclaimed study series of all time, has sold more than 1,000,000 copies in four years. It is used in colleges, high schools and junior highs and by parents and students throughout the world. And Ron has appeared on hundreds of radio and TV shows and countless newspaper and magazine articles and profiles again and again to trumpet his message: Study Smarter, Not Harder!

Here are just a few of the things reviewers have said about *Ron Fry's* **HOW TO STUDY** *Program:*

"These books belong in every secondary library and perhaps in every English classroom. **Highly recommended.**"
— *Library Materials Guide*, Christian Schools International

"Fry's **lively style of writing** makes the book **very useful**."
— *Library Journal*

"Fry has an **appealing, down-to-earth style** that makes this text **accessible and practical.** A regular classroom teacher could extract pertinent lessons to prepare all students to be more successful scholars. The Series would also be appropriate for self-study by college students."
— *Intervention* magazine

"...**approachable, chatty and interactive.** Fry speaks directly to the reader in an **encouraging and sympathetic** fashion it will benefit students from high school age on up."
— *Kliatt Young Adult Paperback Guide*

"...I really liked *How to Study*. **A great gift** for any student."
— *Bookviews*

"Wow! This guy makes sense, he's funny, and he is easy to read. I got the feeling this approach might even work for me!"
— Virginia Meldrum, owner of the Owl's Tree bookstore

"This series **could be useful in resource rooms, in a regular classroom setting or as a self-study guide."**
— Learning Disabilities Association of Canada

Table of

CONTENTS

A MOMENT OF YOUR TIME PLEASE

All of the now-seven titles in my **HOW TO STUDY** *Program* were originally written, or so I thought at the time, for high school students. But over the years I've discovered that the students buying these books are either already in college (which says wonderful things about the preparation they got in high school), in junior high (which says something much more positive about their motivation and, probably, eventual success) or returning to college (about whom more later).

Many of you reading this are adults. Some of you are returning to school. And some of you are long out of school but have figured out that if you could learn *now* the study skills your teachers never taught you, you will do better in your careers.

All too many of you are parents with the same lament: "How do I get Johnny (Janie) to do better in school? He (she) should be getting As but seems to be happy getting Cs."

So I want to briefly take the time to address every one of the audiences for this book and discuss some of the factors particular to each of you:

If you're a high school student

You should be particularly comfortable with both the language and format of the book—its relatively short sentences and paragraphs, occasionally humorous (hopefully) headings and subheadings, a reasonable but certainly not outrageous vocabulary. I wrote it with you in mind! If you can learn to manage your time now, I guarantee you will write me gushy letters of appreciation for years to come. You *will* learn how incredibly valuable these time management tools are...in time.

If you're a junior high school student

You are trying to learn how to study at *precisely* the right time. Sixth, seventh and eighth grades—before that sometimes cosmic leap to high school—is without a doubt the period in which all these study skills should be mastered, since doing so will make high school not just easier but a far more positive and successful experience. Although written for high school-level readers, if you're serious enough about studying to be reading this book, I doubt you'll have trouble with the concepts or the language. You're probably not so busy that you need to fully utilize the time-management tools in this book quite yet, but think how wonderful it will be to be prepared long before you *do* need to use them!

If you're a "traditional" college student...

...somewhere in the 18 to 25 age range, I would have hoped you had already mastered most if not all of the basic study skills. Since you haven't, please make learning, using and mastering all of the study skills covered in my **HOW TO STUDY** *Program* an absolute priority. Do not pass "Go." Do not go on a date. Take the time to learn these skills now. You may have found the time to glide through high school and into college, but I can guarantee if you *don't* master the time-management skills in this book, you will glide right *out* of college in the near future! The pace is simply too quick, the expectations too high, the requirements too time-consuming.

If you're the parent of a student of any age

You must be convinced of one incontestable fact: It is highly unlikely that your child's school is doing anything to teach him or her how to study. *Especially* time management, arguably one of two of the most basic study skills (the other being reading).

How do I know? I spend a lot of time talking to students and visiting schools. And the lack of study skills training is woefully obvious, whether the school is in the poorest section of town or the richest, in the inner city or suburban heaven, public or private, elementary, junior high or high school.

Don't for a minute underestimate the importance of *your* commitment to your child's success: Your involvement in your child's education is absolutely essential to his or her eventual success. Surprisingly enough, the results of every study done in the last two decades about what affects a child's success in school concludes that only one factor *overwhelmingly* affects it, every time: the involvement of the child's parents. Not the size of the school, the money spent per pupil, the number of language labs, how many members of the student body go on to college, how many great teachers there are (or lousy ones). All of these are factors, yes. *But none of them are as significant as the effect **you** can have.*

And even if you were an absolutely *lousy* student, time management may well be the *one* study skill you have been forced to learn in the meantime, just to keep up with your life. So you can have a very positive effect on your child's education, just by teaching him or her what you already know.

So please, take the time to read this book (and all of the others in the series, but especially *How to Study)* yourself. Learn what your kids *should* be learning. (And which of the other five subject-specific books in the series your child needs the most.)

Even if you think you or your child need help only in a single area—or two or three—don't use only the specific book in my program that highlights that subject. Read *How to Study*, *all the way through.* First of all, it will undoubtedly help you increase your mastery of skills you thought you already had. And it will cover those you need help with in a more concise manner. With that background, you will get *more* out of whichever of the other six books you use.

Presuming you need all the help all seven books can give you, what order should you read them in? Aside from reading *How to Study* first—all the way through—I don't think it matters. All of the study skills are interrelated, so practicing one already helps you with the others. If pushed, however, I will admit that I would probably suggest *Improve Your Reading* and *Manage Your Time* be the first two books you study. The former because reading is the basis of every other study skill, the latter because organization is the foundation on which the study pyramid is erected. After that, take your pick!

If you're a nontraditional student

If you're going back to high school, college or graduate school at age 25, 45, 65 or 85—you probably need the help these seven books offer more than anyone! Why? Because the longer you've been out of school, the more likely you don't remember what you've forgotten. And you've forgotten what you're supposed to remember! As much as I emphasize that it's rarely too early to learn good study habits, I must also emphasize that it's never too *late*.

Why you're holding a new edition

I first wrote *How to Study* in 1988, convinced that schools were doing a lousy job of teaching kids how to study—synonymous, to me, with teaching them how to *learn*—and that no one was picking up the slack. (I was also convinced—and still am—that most kids wanted *desperately* to learn but would, without some help, find it easier to fail. And failure, once welcomed, is a nasty habit to break.)

Published in 1989, most bookstores wedged one or two copies of *How to Study* in between the hundreds of phone book-sized test prep volumes. Career Press wasn't a big enough publisher to convince the "chains"—Waldenbooks, Barnes & Noble, B. Dalton—to stock it in any quantity or rich enough to spend any money promoting it.

Need will out. Tens of thousands of people who obviously needed *How to Study* ferreted out copies wherever they lurked and bought them. In 1990, the chains—who *are* smart enough to at least spot a winner the *second* time around—bought 6-copy "prepacks" and gave the book a little more prominence. (Meaning you didn't have to get a hernia removing other books to find a copy of *Study*.) Career Press sent me around the country to appear on radio and TV, including CNN. And hundreds of newspapers and magazines noticed what we were doing and started writing about *How to Study*. (The fact that test scores had declined for the hundred-fortieth year in a row or so probably had something to do with this, but who am I to quibble with the attention?)

In 1991, *booksellers* started calling to say they hoped I was planning some follow-up books to *Study*. And hundreds of parents and students wrote or called to indicate they needed more help in some specific areas. *Ron Fry's* **HOW TO STUDY** *Program* was born, featuring a second edition of *Study* and four new books— *Improve Your Reading, Manage Your Time, Take Notes and Write Papers*—that delved even deeper into critical study skills. That year I spent more time on the phone doing radio shows than I did, I think, with my wife and 2-year-old daughter.

In 1992, I added two more volumes—*"Ace" Any Test* and *Improve Your Memory*, both of which were pretty much written in response to readers' letters. Surprisingly, *Test* and *Memory* quickly became the second- and third-biggest sellers of the seven books in the series, beaten only by *How to Study.* Evidently, my readers knew darned well what they were requesting.

By the way, in both 1992 and 1993, I added mightily to my Frequent Flyer accounts while talking to people nationwide about studying. I wound up visiting 50 cities, some twice, and appearing on more TV and radio shows than are listed in your daily newspaper.

The result of all this travel was twofold: First, sales of all seven books have skyrocketed, in part because of the chance I've been given to talk about them on so many shows and in so many newspapers and magazines. Second, I got to meet and talk with tens of thousands of students and parents, many of whom confirmed the ongoing need for these books *because very little has changed since I first wrote* **How to Study** *some six years ago.*

Test scores of every kind are lower today than they were then. More and more students are dropping out or, if they *do* manage to graduate high school, are finding they are not equipped to do *any*thing, whether they're hoping to go to college or trying to land a job. And more and more parents are frustrated by their children's inability to learn and their schools' seeming inability to teach.

With so much new feedback, it was time to revise all seven books, all of which are being published in time for "back to school" in 1994. In every book, I've included additional topics and expanded on others. I've changed some examples, simplified some, eliminated some. I've rewritten sentences, paragraphs or entire sections that students seemed to be struggling with. Most importantly, I've tried to reflect my new understanding of just who is reading these books—"traditional" students, their parents *and* nontraditional (i.e. older, perhaps much older) students, many of those self-same parents—and write in such a way to include all three audiences.

A couple of caveats

Before we get on with all the tips and techniques you need to take outstanding notes on any topic from any source, let me make two important points about all seven study books.

First, I believe in gender equality, in writing as well as in life. Unfortunately, I find constructions such as "he and she," "s/he," "womyn" and other such stretches to be painfully awkward. I have therefore attempted to sprinkle pronouns of both genders throughout the text. Some teachers, for example, are "he," some are "she." I think this is preferable to using the masculine pronoun throughout but proclaiming one's feminist leanings or to creating so-called "gender-neutral" words or phrases that I find inhibit the "flow" I try to achieve in my writing.

Second, you will find many pieces of advice, examples, lists and other words, phrases and sections spread throughout two or more of the seven books. Certainly *How to Study*, which is an overview of all the study skills, necessarily contains, though in summarized form, some of each of the other six books. But there are discussions of note-taking in *Write Papers* and *Take Notes*, tips about essay tests in *"Ace" Any Test* and *Write Papers*, time management techniques in *Manage Your Time* and *Improve Your Reading*.

The repetition is unavoidable. While I urge everyone to read all seven books in the series, but especially *How to Study*, they *are* seven individual books. And many people only buy one of them. Consequently, I must include in each the pertinent material *for that topic*, even if that material is then repeated in a second or even a third book. As I will point out again and again throughout all the books, these study skills are intimately interrelated.

In many cases, not only is the same topic covered, but it is covered in the same language or uses the same example. If I am particularly happy with the way I covered a subject in one book, I have not gone out of my way to completely rewrite a sentence, paragraph or, for that matter, a whole section just to say it "differently" in another. (Besides, for those who follow my advice and work with all seven books, I think the repetition of some of the important points can only help them learn it more quickly and easily.)

That said, I can guarantee that the nearly 1,000 pages of my *HOW TO STUDY Program* contain the most wide-ranging, comprehensive and complete system of studying ever published. I have attempted to create a system that is usable, that is useful, that is practical, that is learnable. One that *you* can use—whatever your age, whatever your level of achievement, whatever your IQ—to start doing better in school *immediately*.

I hope after reading these books you'll agree I've succeeded.

I'm sure after reading these books that *you'll* succeed.

Ron Fry
May, 1994

MAKE TIME TO STUDY SMARTER

Jim's alarm jolts him awake at 6 a.m.

Because his job keeps him up until midnight most week-nights, he schedules most of his study time for the mornings before classes. And makes sure he never takes a class before 10 a.m.

Unfortunately (for his grades), most mornings he's so tired, he just automatically punches the snooze alarm and sleeps at least another hour.

On a *good* morning, he drags himself out of bed and sits down at his desk to study.

Today seems to be a good morning. He's up by 7, has two cups of coffee, and opens his business ethics text. But Jim, who recognized long ago that he was *not* a morning person, finds his attention wandering. All too soon, he ends up nestling his head on his book and nodding off...until his roommate shakes him awake and informs him he's already late for his first class.

Maybe it wasn't going to be such a good morning after all.

Jim's classes end around 1 p.m. He treats himself to lunch in the student union building and, afterward, to an hour of video games. "I deserve a break," he convinces himself. "This day has been totally frustrating so far."

Despite his best efforts, he feels guilty anyway, because he isn't using his free time to study. By 2:30, with only a couple of hours left before he has to go to work, he reluctantly leaves the video arcade. He's falling further behind in his classes every day, so he *knows* he has to use the rest of the afternoon for studying.

Filled with resolve to catch up on all of his school work before he goes to his job, he heads for the library. As he walks, he begins to mentally catalog the various readings, papers and tests he has to work on. He quickly slows his pace when it suddenly dawns on him that catching up before the end of the *term* would require five or six hours of studying...every day...including weekends.

By the time he gets to the library to study, he's discouraged again. Obviously, anything he can do in the next two hours is a minuscule drop in the bucket compared to what has to be done. Nevertheless, he resolves to do at least a little bit.

As he pulls out his books, a scrap of note paper flutters out. It's the piece of paper he wrote his history assignment on two weeks ago...the term paper that's due in two days!

Not only has he not started it yet, his history book is back at his apartment. He decides he'd better run home to get it—the next two hours is the only time he has to work on it before it's due.

On his way home, he runs into a friend. The two of them commiserate about their impossible schedules. By the time Jim finally gets home, he's decided to ask for an extension on his history assignment. It'll be the second extension he's asked for, which means he's got *two* overdue assignments, one other term paper and four finals to prepare for...in the next two weeks.

There's one hour left. "How can I do a paper in 60 minutes?" Jim groans. Deciding he can't, he throws his book bag on his desk and surrenders to the time pressures. There's no way he can get any real studying done in just an *hour*. He crumples on the couch, turns on the TV, and, as the audience gasps at the sight of a 350-lb transvestite sumo wrestler on "Oprah", asks himself, "Why is *my* life so difficult?"

It's just a matter of time

For Jim, school has become a burden, a time-eating monster that has taken control of his life.

Jim isn't a particularly bad or unusual student. He isn't irresponsible or lazy. He really does want to do well, to get good grades, to prepare himself for a successful career. He's just run out of time.

Let's face it: We all experience problems with time.

We can't speed it up or slow it down.

We need more of it. And don't know where to find it.

Then we wonder where it all went.

But *time* is not really the problem. Time, after all, is the one "currency" that all people are given in equal supply, every day. The problem is that most of us simply let too much of it "slip through our fingers"—because we have *never been taught how to* **manage** *our time.* Our parents never sat us down to give us a little "facts of time" talk. And time management skills aren't part of any standard academic curriculum.

Not knowing how to effectively manage our time, we just continue to use the "natural" approach.

Just act naturally

The natural approach to time is to simply take things as they come and do what you feel like doing, without schedule or plan. What the heck—it worked when we were kids. It was easy to live from day to day and never really worry about "where our time went."

You played when you felt like playing—you didn't make *appointments* to play with your friends. There were no *deadlines*—if your model airplane or doll house didn't get done by the end of the week, no problem. You didn't even *own* a calendar—if you had a piano recital coming up, it was your mom's responsibility to remind you to practice, make sure your good clothes were cleaned and drive you to the recital hall on time.

In fact, sometimes there seemed to be too *much* time—too many *hours* before school was over...too many *days* before summer vacation...too many *weeks* before birthdays...too many *years* before we could learn to drive.

Childhood was a simpler time.

Unfortunately for all of us Peter Pans, there comes a point—too soon, perhaps—when the "take-every-day-as-it-comes" approach just doesn't work. For most of us, it hits in high school. (If you're in high school and don't know what I'm talking about, don't worry—you'll find out your first day of college.)

Why? Because that's when we begin to establish goals that are important to *us,* not just to our parents.

We become more involved in extracurricular activities, such as sports, music or clubs, and must schedule practice times, games and meetings, while still fulfilling our class obligations and home responsibilities.

In college, we begin thinking about our careers. We take classes that will prepare us for that career, may even try to find a part-time job or internship to give us some exposure to it.

To achieve our goals, whether it's performing in the annual school musical or becoming an architect, we must commit ourselves to the many and varied steps it takes to get there.

We must plan. We must *manage* our time.

Whether you're a high school student just starting to feel frazzled, a college student juggling five classes and a part-time job or a parent working, attending classes and raising a family, a simple, easy-to-follow time management system is crucial to your success. And, despite your natural inclination to proclaim that you just don't have the *time* to spend scheduling, listing and recording, it's also the best way to give yourself *more* time.

"Harder" isn't the word I'm thinking of

I'm sure many of you reading this are struggling with your increasing responsibilities and commitments. Some of you, like Jim, may be so overwhelmed you've just given up. Those of you who haven't probably figure it's your fault—if you just worked *harder*, spent more time on your papers and assignments, set up camp in the library—then everything would work out.

So you resign yourselves to frequent all-nighters, to cramming for tests and forgetting about time-consuming activities like eating and sleeping. Trying to do everything—even when there's too much to do—without acquiring the skills to *control* your time, is an approach that will surely lead to burn out.

When does it all end?

With classes, homework, a part-time or full-time job, and all the opportunities for fun and recreation, life as a high school or young college student can be very busy. But, believe me, it *doesn't* suddenly get *easier* when you graduate.

Most adults will tell you that it only gets *busier*. There will always be a boss who expects you to work later, children who need to be fed, clothed, and taken to the doctor, hobbies and interests to pursue, community service to become involved in, courses to take.

If you're an adult doing all of the latter, I sure don't have to tell you how important time management is, do I?

There may *not* be enough time for *every*thing

When I asked one busy student if she wished she had more time, she joked, "I'm *glad* there are only 24 hours in a day. Any more and I wouldn't have an excuse for not getting everything done!"

Let me give you the good news: There *is* a way that you can accomplish more in less time, one that's a *lot* more effective than the natural approach. And it doesn't even take more effort. You can plan ahead and make conscious choices about how your time will be spent, and how much time you will spend on each task. You can have more control over your time, rather than always running out of time as you keep trying to do everything.

Now the bad news: The first step to managing your time should be deciding just what is important...and what isn't. Difficult as it may be, sometimes its necessary for us to recognize that we truly *can't* do it all. To slice from our busy schedules those activities that aren't as meaningful to us so that we can devote more energy to those that are.

You may be a "Star Trek" fan from way back. But is it really the best use of your time to run back to your room to catch the morning rerun each weekday?

You may love music so much, you want to be in the orchestra, jazz band, choir and play with your own garage band on weekends. But is it realistic to commit to all four?

Your job at the mall boutique may mean 20% off on the clothes you buy. But if you're working there four days a week, taking 15 hours of classes and working at the food co-op on weekends, when do you expect to study?

If you're raising a family, working part-time and trying to take a near-full class load yourself, it's probably time to cure yourself of the Super Mom Syndrome.

But there *is* enough time to plan

Yet, even after paring down our commitments, most of us are still challenged to get it all done. What with classes, study time, work obligations, extracurricular activities and social life, it's not easy getting it all in—even without "Star Trek."

The time management plan that I outline in this book is designed particularly for students. Whether you're in high school, college or graduate school, a "traditional" student or one who's chosen to return to school after being out in the "real world" for awhile, you'll find that this is a manageable program that will work for you.

My time management program allows for flexibility. In fact, I encourage you to adapt any of my recommendations to your own unique needs. That means it will work for you whether you are living in a dorm, sharing accommodations with a roommate, or living with a spouse and children. That you *can* learn how to balance school, work, fun, and even family obligations.

The purpose of this book is to help you make *choices* about what is important to you, to help you set *goals* for yourself, to help you *organize* and *schedule* your time, and to develop the *motivation* and *self-discipline* to follow your schedule and reach those goals.

Which will give you the time to learn all the other study skills I write about!

Chapter One

TAKE THE TIME TO PLAN

"I recommend that you learn to take care of the minutes, for the hours will take care of themselves."
—Lord Chesterfield

What if you never developed a plan for your school curriculum, never even chose a major? What if you just "followed your star," wherever it led, taking whatever subjects you felt like, whenever you felt like going to class?

Perhaps you'd take a business class because you heard Michael Eisner made $200 million last year...*and* got to go on Splash Mountain as often as he wanted.

You have a friend who's majoring in psychology, so you'd take a psychology class with her.

Your dad is an engineer and he seems to like his job, so you'd throw in a basic science course.

You just read *All The President's Men,* so you decide to sign up for a journalism class.

And to round out your schedule, you'd take *any* course that incredibly cute guy is taking, wherever it fits!

If you continue like this for four years, you may have broadened your interests and learned a lot (and/or gotten a boyfriend), but you wouldn't have a degree to show for all your work, and you'd probably find it awfully difficult to find a job when you left school—degreeless, remember?

Planning makes the world go 'round

Consider an even simpler project: Try going grocery shopping without a list. If you're like me and always go food shopping before you've eaten, you'll probably wind up with a cart right out of "junk-food heaven," laden with anything and everything that looks good: soda, chips, sandwich cookies and ice cream.

You might run out of money at the cash register—how could you figure how much money to bring if you had no idea what you were buying?

Worst of all, when you got home, you may discover that you already had *two* packages of sandwich cookies, a refrigerator *full* of soda, two gallons of ice cream clogging up the freezer and enough chips to open a delicatessen.

But you didn't get cat food (she's been living on tuna and cereal for two days, you cur) or milk...or anything for that night's dinner.

Whether your goal is to graduate from college or buy groceries for the week, the need for a plan should be clear.

Just as clear, unfortunately, is the fact that far too many people *do* manage their time like the student without a major or the shopper without a list.

I've got a secret

Just like the grocery list and the school curriculum, setting up a plan for managing your time will take effort. But it's an investment of effort that will bring exponential returns.

Wouldn't it be nice to actually have some *extra* time ...instead of always "running out of it?"

To feel that you're exerting some control over your schedule, your schoolwork, your *life*...instead of caroming from appointment to appointment, class to class, assignment to assignment, like some crazed billiard ball?

It can happen.

I will not spend a lot of time trying to convince you that this is a "fun" idea—getting excited about calendars and "to do" lists is a bit of a stretch. You will *not* wake up one morning and suddenly decide that organizing your life is just the most fun thing you can think of.

But I suspect you *will* do it if I can convince you that effective time management will reward you in some very tangible ways.

Presuming all this is true (and I'll wager it is), unless you have some darn good reasons—a solid idea of some of the benefits effective time management *can* bring you—you probably will find it hard to consistently motivate yourself to do it. It has to become a habit, something you do without thinking, but also something you do *no matter what.*

Yes, I have a few of those good reasons ready to trot out, but before I do so, why don't *you* spend several minutes thinking about the potential benefits effective time management might bring you. If you can already spot the potential rewards in your own life, that's even better than waiting for my reasons! Write your ideas in the spaces on the next page.

How time management can help me

Now I'll give you my list.
See if I thought of anything you didn't.

Short-term benefits

A time management system that fits your needs can help you get more work done in less time. Whether your priority is more free time than you have now or better grades, effective time management can help you reach your objective, because it:

1. *Helps you put first things first.* Have you ever spent an evening doing a busy-work assignment for an *easy* class, only to find that you hadn't spend enough time studying for a crucial test in a more difficult one?

   Listing the tasks that must be done and *prioritizing* them ensures that the most important things will *always* get done—*even when you don't get* everything *done.*

2. *Helps you avoid time traps.* Time traps are the un-planned events that pop up, sometimes (it seems) every day. They're the fires you have to put out be-fore you can turn to tasks like studying.

   You may fall into such time traps because they *seem* urgent...or because they seem *fun.* Or end up spending hours in them...without even realizing you're stuck:

   You blow an hour of study time at the library because you've left the required study materials at home.

   Or sit down in front of the TV to relax while you eat dinner and get caught up in a two-hour movie.

   There is no way to avoid *every* time trap. But effective time management can help you avoid most of them. Time management is like a fire-*prevention* approach rather than a fire-*fighting* one: It allows you to go about your work systematically instead of moving from crisis to crisis or whim to whim.

3. *Helps you anticipate opportunities.* In addition to helping you balance study time with other time de-ands, effective time management can help make the time you *do* spend studying more productive. You will be able to get more done in the same amount of time or (this is even better) do more work in less time. I'm sure you could find *some* way to spend those extra hours each week.

Imagine that two students are working on the same research paper assignment. One student (you, of course), plans out the steps to be completed in advance and starts on them early. Another student delays even thinking about the paper until a week before the assignment is due.

If both students were unable to find all the material they needed in their local library, the one who started early would have the opportunity to send away for it. The student who only had a week left would not have the same luxury. Or the same good grade.

4. *Gives you freedom and control.* Contrary to many students' fears, time management is *liberating,* not restrictive. A certain control over *part* of your day al-lows you to be flexible with the *rest* of your day.

In addition, you will be able to plan freedom into your schedule. For example, you would know in advance that you have a big test the day after a friend's party. Instead of having to call your friend the night of the party with a sob story, you could make sure you allocated enough study time before-hand and go to the party without feeling guilty, without even *thinking* about the test.

5. *Helps you avoid time conflicts.* Have you ever lived the following horror story? You get out of class at 5:30, remember you have a big math assignment due, *then* realize you have no time to do it since you have a music rehearsal at 6 p.m. *Then* you remember that your softball game is scheduled for 7:00...just before that date you made months ago (which you never did remember!).

   Simply having all of your activities, responsibilities and tasks written down in one place helps ensure that two or three things don't get scheduled at once. If time conflicts do arise, you will notice them well in advance and can rearrange things accordingly.

6. *Helps you avoid feeling guilty.* When you know how much studying has to be done and have the time scheduled to do it, you can relax—you *know* that the work will get done. It is much easier to forget about studying if you've already allotted the time for it. Without a plan to finish the work you are doing, you may feel like it's "hanging over your head"—even when you're not working on it. And if you're going to spend time *thinking* about studying, you might as well just spend the time *studying!*

   Effective time management also helps keep your conscience off your back: When your studying is done, you can *really* enjoy your free time *without* feeling guilty because you're not studying.

7. *Helps you evaluate your progress.* If you know where you should be in class readings or assignments, you will never be surprised when deadlines loom. For example, if you've planned out the whole term and

know you have to read an average of 75 pages a week to keep up in your business management class, and you only read *60* pages this week, you don't need a calculator to figure out you are slightly behind. And it's easy enough to schedule a little more time to read next week so you catch up.

On the other hand, if you only read when it's convenient (i.e., when your assignment doesn't conflict with your favorite TV shows) or until you're tired, you'll never know whether you're behind or ahead (but I'll bet you're behind!). Then one day you suddenly realize you have to be up to Chapter 7...by lunch time.

Good time management helps you know where you are and how you're doing...all along the way.

8. *Helps you see the "big picture."* Effective time management provides you with a bird's-eye view of the semester. Instead of being caught off guard when the busy times come, you will be able to plan ahead—*weeks* ahead—when you have big tests or assignments due from more than one class.

Why not complete that German paper a few days early so it's not in the way when two other papers are due...or you're trying to get ready for a weekend ski trip? Conflicts can be worked out with fewer problems if you know about them in advance...and do something to eliminate them.

9. *Helps you see the "bigger picture."* Planning ahead and plotting your course early allows you to see how classes fit with your overall school career. For example, if you know you have to take chemistry, biology,

and pharmacology to be eligible for entrance into the nursing program, and that the courses you will take later will build on those, you will at least be able to see why the classes are required for your major, even if you aren't particularly fond of one or two of them.

"I have to take statistics because my counselor said it was required" is not as strong a motivator as "It's the next-to-last required class before graduation!"

10. *Helps you learn how to study smarter, not harder.* Students sometimes think time management just means reallocating their time—spending the same time studying, the same time in class, the same time partying, just shifting around these "time segments" so everything is more "organized."

As we'll see later in this book, this is only *partially* true—a key part of effective time management *is* learning how to prioritize tasks. But this simple view ignores one great benefit of taking control of your time: It may well be possible you will be *so* organized, *so* prioritized, *so in control of your time* that you can spend *less* time studying, get *better* grades and have *more* time for other things—extracurricular activities, hobbies, a film, whatever.

It's *not* magic, though it certainly can *appear* magical.

Long-term benefits

Besides helping you to manage your time right now and reach your immediate study goals, effective time management will bring long-term benefits.

Have you ever sat in a class and thought to yourself, "I'll *never* use this stuff once I get out of school?"

You won't say that about time management skills. They will be useful throughout your life.

Learning time management skills now will help you prepare for the future. Preparation is what school is all about—if you spend your time effectively now, you will be better prepared for the future.

And the better prepared you are, the more options you will have—effective learning and good grades *now* will increase your range of choices when you graduate. The company you work for or the graduate school you attend will be one *you* choose, not one whose choice was dictated by your poor past performance.

Learning how to manage your time now will develop habits and skills you can use outside of school. It may be difficult for you to develop the habits of effective time management, but don't think you're alone—time management presents just as much of a problem to many parents, professors, and non-students. How many people do you know who *never* worry about time?

If you learn effective time management skills in school, the payoffs will come throughout your life. Whether you wind up running a household or a business, you will have learned skills you will use every day.

Consider the examples of Sam and Taylor, both business executives at a large company. Sam has difficulty managing his time; in fact, he often feels controlled by his job. He's always running to get office supplies to complete a report or gets caught in long, unproductive phone conversations with clients, working on the details of some low-priority task or doing busy work that other people have asked him to do.

The result: A desk always stacked with unfinished (and more important) work. Which means he often has to stay late to finish a report or take work home because he just didn't have time to finish that big presentation or important project when it should have been done—at work.

Taylor, on the other hand, makes a list of weekly priorities every Monday morning and is careful about committing to any projects for which her list clearly shows she doesn't have the time. Instead of spending all her time putting out fires, handling crises, and doing work that she could delegate to someone else, she refers to her priority list often and *always* does the most important things first.

She is realistic and knows that she will never be able to do *everything* she would like. But because she plans, she gets the important projects done...on time. And her boss knows she can count on Taylor to handle extra, emergency assignments.

At the end of the day, Taylor usually feels satisfied that she did a good job. And, at the end of the week, rather than worrying about leftover tasks that need to be handled on Saturday or Sunday, she can relax and enjoy her weekend. In fact, she sometimes takes a Friday afternoon off to go to the beach.

Her relaxed weekends, in turn, make her even more effective when she returns to work Monday mornings.

I'm not David Copperfield

Time management is not a magic wand that can be waved to solve problems in school or after graduation. It is not as much a talent as a craft. There is no "time management gene" that you either have or lack, like the ones that produce brown eyes or black hair.

These techniques are tools that can be used to help you reach your short-term and long-range goals successfully.

The important thing to remember is that you *can* be a successful time manager and a successful student *if* you are willing to make the effort to learn and apply the principles in this book.

Chapter Two

SPEND TIME TO SAVE TIME

Some people groan aloud when they hear the words "time management." They imagine distressingly organized individuals armed with endless lists, charts and graphs, chained to a rigid schedule, with no room (or time!) for fun.

If you hate the idea of being tied to a schedule, if you fear that it would drain all spontaneity and fun from your life, I know you'll be pleasantly surprised when you discover that just the *opposite* is true:

Most students are relieved and excited when they learn what a liberating tool time management can be.

Let's explode some of the myths that may be holding *you* back.

Time management myths

Let's look at some of the fears some of you may have about "time management", *fears which are groundless.*

Save me from my schedule

Inflexibility is most people's biggest fear—"If I set it all out on a schedule, then I won't be able to be spontaneous and choose what to do with my time later."

Your time management system can be as flexible as you want. In fact, the best systems act as guides, not some rigid set of "must do's" and "can't do's."

I'm captain of the Time Patrol

Contrary to common belief, time management skills will not turn you into a study-bound bookworm or time-crunching fanatic. How much time do you need to set aside for studying? Ask your career counselor, and he or she will probably echo the timeworn "2:1 ratio"—spend two hours studying *out* of class for every hour you spend *in* class.

Hogwash. That ratio may be way out of line—either not enough time or too much. The amount of study time will vary from individual to individual, depending on your major, your abilities, needs and goals.

Scheduling time to study doesn't mean that you have to go from three hours of studying a day to eight. In fact, laying out your study time in advance often means you can relax more when you're *not* studying because you won't be worrying about when you're going to get your schoolwork done—the time's been set aside.

How *long* you study is less important than how *effective* you are when you do sit down to study.

Manage Your Time

The time management skills in this book are designed to help you get the most out of your study time. The goal is not to spend *more* time studying, but to spend the same or less time, *getting more done in* whatever *time you spend.*

It's too darned involved

Many of you fear the complexity time *management* implies. Actually, I recommend simplicity. The more complex your system becomes, the harder it will be to use and, consequently, the less likely you *will* use it consistently. The more complex the system, the more likely it will collapse.

I, robot

You can design your time management system to fit your own needs. Some of the skills you will learn in this book will be more helpful to you in reaching your goals than others. You may already be using some of them. Others you will want to start using right now. Still others may not fit your needs at all.

Use the skills that seem the most likely to lead you to *your* study goals, meet *your* needs, and fit with *your* personality.

For example, two excellent students I know approach study and time management in nearly opposite ways.

Alison plans out almost every detail of her morning and afternoon, scheduling long blocks of time for study, work and other tasks. On the other hand, she leaves her evenings flexible and, when she goes out, her schedule behind.

Tim prefers to work throughout the day, scheduling all of his activities in smaller blocks of time. He could never spend eight straight hours doing schoolwork, as Alison often does. He also has smaller blocks of free time scattered throughout the day and evening.

Are you like Tim? Like Alison?

Sort of a mix?

Doesn't matter. What *does* is that as long as their systems work for each of them, there is nothing inherently right or wrong, good or bad, about either.

They *work.*

Time management realities

So much for the myths and fears. Let's look at what is actually required to use time management skills effectively:

A good notebook and a sharp pencil

In order for time management to work, you have to be able to look at your plan when it's time to use it. It's nearly impossible to make detailed plans very far in advance without having a permanent record. Make it your rule: "If I plan it out, I will write it down." And, preferably, write your plans and schedules for every week and school term in one place so you always know where to find them.

I've provided some schedule formats in Chapter 8 for you to photocopy and use. They've been effective for me. (I'll cover them in greater detail in later chapters.) There are a myriad of other schedule planners available in bookstores and office supply stores—you can even create your own on notebook paper.

What's important is that you have *one place to write and keep all your schedule information*, including class times, meetings, study times, project due dates, vacations, doctor appointments and social events.

41

Your readiness to adapt and personalize

The time management system that best suits you will be one that is tailor-made to fit *your* needs and personality. Many of the approaches included in this book are general suggestions that work well for many people, but that doesn't mean each one will be right for you.

Consider the following example: While most parents turn the lights out and keep things quiet when their baby is trying to go to sleep, one baby I know, who spent two months in the hustle and bustle of a newborn intensive-care unit, couldn't sleep unless the lights were *on* and it was *noisy.*

Similarly, while many students will study best in a quiet environment, others may feel uncomfortable in a "stuffy" library and prefer studying in their living room.

Make your study schedule work for *you,* not your night-owl roommate who must plan every activity down to the minute. Alter it, modify it, make it stricter, make it more flexible. Whatever works.

Regular attention and consistent use

We've all had the experience of missing an important appointment or commitment and saying, "I know I had that written down somewhere—I wonder *where!*"

It's easy to *think,* "I'll write it down so I won't forget," but a schedule that is not used regularly isn't a safety net at all. You must *consistently* write down your commitments. You must spend time filling out your schedule every week, every day.

Any efforts you make to manage your time will be futile if you do not have your schedule with you when you need it. For example, you are in art class without your schedule when your teacher tells you when your next project is due. You jot it down in your art notebook and promise yourself you'll add it to your schedule as soon as you get home.

You hurry to your next class, and your geology instructor schedules a study session for the following week. You scribble a reminder in your lab book.

Between classes, a friend stops to invite you to a party Thursday night. You promise you'll be there.

You arrive at work to find out your supervisor has scheduled your hours for the following week. She checks them with you, they seem fine, so you commit to them.

Had you been carrying your schedule with you, you would have been able to write down your art project and schedule the necessary amount of preparation time.

You would have realized that your geology study session was the same night as your friend's party.

And discovered that accepting the work schedule your supervisor presented left you with little time to work on your art project.

Take your schedule with you anywhere and everywhere you think you might need it.

When in doubt, take it along!

Keeping your schedule with you will reduce the number of times you have to say, "I'll just try to remember it for now" or "I'll write it down on this little piece of paper and transfer it to my planner later."

Always make a point of writing down tasks, assignments, phone numbers, and other bits of important information in your schedule *immediately*.

A trial run

In order to test its effectiveness, you must give any time management system a chance to work—give it a trial run. No program can work unless it is utilized consistently. And consistency won't happen without effort.

It's just like learning to ride a bicycle. It's a pain at first; you may even fall down a few times. But once you're a two-wheel pro, you can travel much faster and farther than you could by foot.

The same goes for the techniques you will learn here—they may take practice and a little getting used to, but once you have maintained a time management program for a couple of weeks, you will probably find yourself in the habit of doing it. From then on, it will take relatively little effort to maintain.

That's when you'll really notice the payoff—when the task becomes second nature.

Chapter Three

SET THE STAGE FOR SUCCESS

Stacey gets home from work and fixes a sandwich. It's been a long, tiring day. It's after 5 p.m. and she knows she has to start her homework. Sandwich in hand, she clears a spot on the table between the breakfast dishes and gets out her books. She starts to read but finds it difficult to concentrate. She reads off and on as she finishes her sandwich.

"It's the dishes!" she concludes, holding the dirty dishes responsible for diverting her attention from her studies. She decides to take a break to wash them. Twenty minutes later, Stacey sits down at a clear table.

Five minutes after *that,* however, her mother arrives home from work and begins preparing dinner. Stacy tries to read as her mother cuts vegetables and asks Stacey questions about an upcoming dance.

A half-hour later, after they've finished planning a dress-shopping trip, Stacey can see that her study efforts aren't working. She clears her books off the table so her mother can set it for dinner, and vows to stay up past midnight, if necessary, to get her reading done.

It's obvious that, despite Stacey's motivation to study, she just seemed to be in the *wrong* place at the *wrong* time. That's exactly how many of *you* probably feel when the elements of your study environment are working against you.

What's *your* best study environment?

There is no one right combination of factors that constitutes a perfect study environment for everyone. However, in order to be effective, you must find the combinations of place and time that work for you.

Of all the suggestions and techniques discussed in this book, careful attention to *where* and *when* you study is probably the simplest and easiest to apply. And the right mix will make a big difference in your productivity.

Unlike Stacey, Kay studies at her desk. She keeps all her materials nearby, avoiding needless trips to other rooms of the house.

She keeps the desk itself clear of books and paper piles so she can spread out her work and study comfortably.

The area is well lit, so she rarely has problems with headaches or eyestrain.

Finally, because she studies in an area removed from the activity of the rest of the house, she is rarely interrupted by others...or distracted by things like the television, telephone or dirty dishes.

Who do *you* think gets more done in less time?

Where should *you* study?

At the library. And realize within the library there may be numerous choices, from the large reading room, to quieter, sometimes deserted specialty rooms, to your own study cubicle. My favorite "home away from home" at Princeton was a little room that seemingly only four or five of us knew about—with four wonderfully comfortable chairs, subdued lighting, phonographs with earplugs and a selection of some 500 classical records. For someone who needs music to study, the room was custom-made for me!

At home. Just remember that this is the place where distractions are most likely to occur. No one tends to telephone you at the library and little brothers (or your own kids) will not tend to find you easily in the "stacks." It is, of course, usually the most convenient place to make your study headquarters. It may not, however, be the most effective.

At a friend's, neighbor's or relative's. This may not be an option at all for most of you, even on an occasional basis, but you may want to set up one or two alternative study sites. Despite many experts' opinion that you must study in the same place every night (with which I don't agree), I have a friend who simply craves some variety to help motivate him. He has four different places he likes to study and simply rotates them from night to night. Whatever works for you.

In an empty classroom. Certainly an option at many colleges and perhaps some private high schools, it is an interesting idea mainly because so few students have ever thought of it! While not a likely option at a public high school, it never hurts to ask if you can't make some arrangements. Since many athletic teams practice until 6 p.m. or later, even on the high school level, there may well be a part of the school open—and usable with permission—even if the rest is locked up tight.

At your job. Whether you are a student working part-time or working full-time and going to school part-time, you may be able to make arrangements to use an empty office, even during regular office hours, perhaps after everyone has left (depending on how much your boss trusts you). If you're in junior high or high school and a parent, friend or relative works nearby, you may be able to work from just after school until closing time at their workplace.

A place just for study

Psychologists know that you can often predict human behavior accurately if you know just one thing: the individual's environment at the time. We are conditioned to behave in certain ways based on specific cues from our environments.

Not only are certain environments cues for specific behaviors, the *more* we behave a certain way in a given environment, the *stronger* that tendency becomes. Repetition is the way habits are formed.

Consider the example of a dog. What would the environmental cue of a plastic saucer lead a dog to do?

It all depends on what he has done in the past with that saucer. If it's his food dish, setting it out may make his mouth water. But if his owner usually uses it to play "catch" with him, he may jump about playfully when he sees it.

How about you? What does your pillow suggest to you? "Sleep" should be your immediate response. So if you study on your bed, propped up by your pillows, you may find yourself falling asleep soon after you open your books. In fact, if you study regularly in your bed, you may eventually not be able to sleep well there!

If possible, designate an area in your room or house that is *just for studying.* You will eventually condition yourself to the extent that just sitting down at your desk will help you gear up for studying.

In order to get to this point, however, you will have to make sure you do not allow your mind to become conditioned to other things while at your study desk or table. If you feel tired or are finding it difficult to concentrate, don't put your head down on your *desk* to rest or daydream. If you need a break, get up and rest in an easy chair or on your bed. Or go take a walk.

If you physically get up and leave your study area when you're not studying, you'll help strengthen the conditioning message: "This desk is only for studying."

Make it pleasant

It helps to make your desk or study area a *positive* place to study. For example, to create a motivating atmosphere, you may want to put up pictures of your dream job to help you remember *why* you're subjecting yourself to these long hours of study and homework.

And don't push yourself to study for unbearable lengths of time. Few things will make you dislike school more than studying until you are sick of the subject matter and your head aches.

Take your own stamina into account. Some people can plop down in a chair, open a book and read or study for hours. Others find their mind wandering after an hour or two. The former doesn't need a break. The latter, if he or she wants to effectively study after that first hour or two, better schedule short breaks accordingly. Remember: Your study plan should be flexible. Adapt it to *your* needs, strengths and weaknesses.

Avoid distractions

Consider the location of your desk or study area. Is it in a high-traffic area, where family members or roommates are likely to be walking through, watching TV or eating? Is it by a window where you can be distracted by passersby or easily daydream because of the wonderful view? The best position for a desk is usually in a quiet, low-traffic area—for example, in a corner or facing a wall. There might not be much of a view, but there won't so many easy ways to be distracted, either.

Make it convenient

The perfect study environment, an area meeting all of the above criteria, may not be readily accessible to you. A commitment to always study at the library isn't realistic if the library is 10 miles away and you don't have a car.

If you have a two-hour free period between work and class, but it takes you a half-hour to drive home to your study desk, you'd do better to find a quiet coffee shop to read a couple of chapters, even if it isn't as ideal as your own area.

Your study spot should be *accessible* and *convenient.*

Have more than one place

Or maybe I should say your study *spots.*

You may be a student who can (or must) study in a variety of locations, depending on the demands of your schedule. You may want to study in a doctor's office lobby or while you're waiting for an appointment with a professor. Or maybe in the car while you're waiting to pick up your spouse from work or as you carpool to school.

Even if you have one primary study location, occasional changes may be required because of circumstance. Your room and its big oak roll-top desk may be your dream study environment. But if you spend a lot of time on campus—which is a 20-minute drive from home—you'll want to scout out a nice, quiet corner of the library to call your second "study home."

"Do not disturb"

It may help to keep a real or imaginary barrier between you and the outside world while you're studying. Shutting the door to your room helps block out noise and prevents many intrusions. A "please do not disturb" sign is a great way of telling people you are busy. One student had a pair of Halloween-costume alien antenna he wore whenever he was studying—a friendly reminder to himself and his roommates that he wished to be left alone. In addition to the message you send to other people, the physical act of putting on your "thinking cap" can be a great conditioner—it will put you in the "study mood."

All elements of your study environment

Environment is more than location. Whether you primarily study at school, at home, in the library or in your car, there are other elements of a study environment that can inhibit or facilitate studying.

Are you in a comfortable chair? It should be pleasant to sit in, though perhaps not as relaxing as a recliner!

What about ventilation and temperature? Does your study spot become stuffy and hot, or so cold you have to wear gloves?

What about keeping the radio or TV on while you're studying? Some people—myself included—work better with a little music in the background, and literally find it *more* difficult to work when it's too quiet. (Though I don't know anyone who works better with the Stones at 90 decibels or while watching "Jeopardy"!)

Before you decide this matter for yourself, you may want to time yourself to see how much you can accomplish without music, then time yourself with music playing. If you feel that music is a positive influence in your study environment, go ahead and play it, but remember that certain types of music are more conducive to studying than others. Familiar tunes, with a steady rhythm, are less distracting than songs with lyrics, a variety of rhythms and, of course, high decibel levels.

Give your studies the time of day

We've talked about the importance of *place* when you study, and that you should create the *habit* of studying in the same place or places. The same goes for *when* you study as well. As much as possible, create a routine time of day you study. Some students find it easier to set aside specific blocks of time during the day, each day, they plan on studying. In reality, the time of day you will do your work will be determined by a number of factors. Consider the following:

1. *Study when you're at your best.* What is your "peak performance period"—the time of day you do your best work? This varies from person to person—you may be dead to the world 'til noon but able to study well into the night. Or up and alert at the crack of dawn but distracted and tired if you try to burn the midnight oil.

Figure out the time of day you find it easiest to concentrate and are able to get the most done and, whenever possible, plan to do your most difficult work then.

Keep in mind that for most people, there are some times of the day when it is particularly difficult to concentrate on anything—right after a big meal, for example, much of your blood goes to your stomach to work on digesting the food. You may find yourself less alert if you try to study then.

2. *Consider your sleep habits.* Habit is a powerful influence. If you always set your alarm for 7 a.m., you may find that you wake up then even when you forget to set it. If you are used to going to sleep around 11 p.m., you will undoubtedly get quite tired if you try to stay up studying until 2 a.m. And probably accomplish little in the three extra hours.

   Although sleep is a physical necessity influenced by biorhythms as well as habitual behavior, we become conditioned to perform certain activities at certain times of the day.

   Which is why it is difficult to adjust to a new study time when you start a new schedule and try to study during hours you have previously been sleeping.

   It's tempting to take those big blank spots in your late-night or early-morning schedule and plan to study. But if you're used to *sleeping* at those times, you'll probably find it difficult to focus on your studies. Try as you might, you'll likely wind up just using your history book for a pillow!

3. *Study when you can.* Although you want to sit down to study when you are mentally most alert, external

factors also play a role in deciding when you study. As I mentioned earlier, some students are not able to study consistently in the same study spot, however ideal it may be. Same with *when* you study. You may be most alert during the late afternoon hours, but if you have to work from 1 p.m. to 5 p.m., you're not going to be able to take advantage of that time to study.

Many other factors influence your available study times. Being at your best is a great goal but not always possible: You must study whenever circumstances allow.

4. *Consider the complexity of the assignment when you allocate time.* The tasks themselves may have a great affect on your schedule. When I sit down to plan out the chapter of a book, for example, I need a relatively long period of uninterrupted time—at least an hour, perhaps as many as three—to get my notes in the order I want them and think through the entire chapter, writing transitions in my head, noting problem areas, figuring out where I need an example or illustration. If I only have half an hour before a meeting or appointment, I wouldn't even attempt to start such a project, since I'd just have to start all over again when I had the right amount of time.

You may find yourself to be the same way and, therefore, need to ensure your schedule is flexible enough to adapt to the demands of the specific task. Fifteen-minute study unit increments might work well for you most of the time (though I suspect half an hour is an ideal unit for most of you, an hour only for those of you who can work that long without a break and who have assignments that traditionally take that long to complete). On the other hand, you may have no problem at all working on a long project in fits and starts, 15 or 20 minutes at a time, without needing to retrace your steps each time you pick it up again.

Collect your study materials

Have you ever sat down to study, only to realize that you needed a calculator from another room? On your way to get it you decide to go through the kitchen to grab a snack. Your roommate is making dinner, and you ask her about her new after-school internship. After a few minutes of chatting, you spot the newspaper on the table and check the headlines. As you head back to your room, you pause in the doorway, wondering, "Now what did I come in here for again?"

Remember time traps? This is one—not having your materials together, which means you have to spend extra time gathering them. You risk getting sidetracked and losing valuable study time.

You can save immense amounts of time simply by keeping your textbooks, pencils and pens, calculator, and other necessities within arm's reach.

Some students like to use a three-ring binder for all their school papers. Lecture notes from each class can be kept together and marked by a tab. Holes can be punched in handouts and other papers from class and then kept with class notes. In addition, semester or quarter calendars, weekly schedules, phone lists and other necessities can all be kept in one place. That way you only have to carry around a single binder, not keep track of four, five, six or more different notebooks or folders.

Manage Your Time

To make sure your binder doesn't get too full or bulky from the semester's work, you can empty the contents occasionally into file folders marked for each class. You may even want to keep a small file holder near your desk to allow quick access to materials from the semester.

If these become too full as school continues and materials accumulate, they can be placed in a larger filing cabinet.

This system will keep your class notes and other useful papers organized and easy to find. As you study from day to day, papers often start stacking up on your desk anyway. Create new folders as necessary to hold them.

There are many different ways you can organize your study space and notebooks. You can buy file cabinets, stack plastic baskets on your desk, invest in an inexpensive packet of multi-colored folders, etc. The important thing is to always have everything you need handy when you're ready to study, whatever system you devise.

Take it with you

If you study away from your home or room, it is doubly important to have everything you need with you. If you are studying in the library and forgot your assignment book, you can't just run to the next room and grab it.

Look over your schedule each morning (we'll discuss your Daily Schedule in detail in Chapter 6) and determine what you will need for the day. If you must study lecture notes from your business class that day, make sure you pack your notes that morning—or, since mornings are so hectic, load your briefcase or book bag the night before.

And don't forget to bring your schedule with you. We've already seen how easily assignments get forgotten if they're not written down immediately!

The more the merrier

If you have materials that you often need *both* at home and at school, it's a good idea to keep a duplicate set of all such essentials at school or in your book bag or briefcase. Or find a locker in the buildings in which you spend the most time. It's comforting to know that you will never be without essential supplies...wherever you're studying.

How are you doing?

Let's find out how well you're doing with the principles in this chapter. Sit down at your desk or study area right now and evaluate your study environment, using the following questions:

1. Do you have one or two special places reserved just for studying? Or do you study wherever seems convenient or available at the time?

2. Is your study area a pleasant place? Would you offer it to a friend as a good place to study? Or do you dread going near it because it's so depressing? (It's hard enough, sometimes, to sit down to study in the first place; a dungeon-like environment just makes it harder.)

3. How's the lighting? Is it too dim or too bright? Is the whole desk well lit? Or only portions of it?

4. Are all the materials you need handy? Do you have writing instruments? Extra lined paper or scratch paper? A calculator? A garbage can? Other needed equipment, such as computer supplies or textbooks?

5. What else do you do here? Eat? Sleep? Write letters or read for pleasure? If you try to study at the same

place you sit to listen to your music or chat on the phone, you may find yourself doing one when you think you're doing the other!

6. Is your study area in a high-traffic or low-traffic area? How often are you interrupted by people passing through?

7. Can you close the door to the room to avoid disturbances and outside noise?

8. When do you spend the most time here? What time of day do you study? Is it when you are at your best, or do you inevitably study when you're tired and less productive?

9. Are your files, folders and other class materials near the work area and organized? Do you have some filing system for them? If you wanted to look at your class notes from last month—or last year—would you know where to quickly find them?

Create *your* ideal environment

On page 67, I have included a checklist for you to rate your study environment. If you don't know the answer to one or more of the questions, take the time to experiment.

Many of the items on this chart should be understandable to you now. Remember: *Why* you feel the need for a particular environment is not important. Knowing that you *have a preference* is. Here's what you're trying to assess in each item (numbered to correspond with those on the chart) and how *your* preferences might affect your study regimen:

1. If you prefer "listening" to "seeing," you'll have little problem getting the information you need from class

lectures and discussion. In fact, you'll *prefer* them to studying your textbooks. (You may have to concentrate on your reading skills and spend more time with your textbooks to offset this tendency. Highlighting your texts may help.)

If you're more of a "visual" person, you'll probably find it easier reading your textbook and may have to work to improve your classroom concentration. Taking excellent class notes that you can read later will probably be important for you.

2. This should tie in with your answer to (1). The more "oral" you are, the more you should concentrate on listening. The more "visual," the better your notes should be for later review.

3. This may make a difference for a number of reasons. You may find it difficult to hear or see from the back of the classroom. You may be shy and want to sit up front to make yourself participate. You may find sitting near a window makes you feel less claustrophobic; alternatively, you may daydream too much if near a window and should sit as far "inside" the classroom as possible.

4. Whatever location you find most conducive to study—given the limitations of your living situation and schedule—should be where you spend the majority of your study time.

5. How to organize your time to most effectively cover the material: This may depend, in part, on the amount of homework you are burdened with and/or the time of year—you may have one schedule during most of the school year but have to adapt during test time, if papers are due, for special projects, etc.

6. To some of you, such preferences may only be a factor on weekends, because your day hours are set—you're in school.

    But if you are in college (or in a high school program that mimics college's "choose your own courses and times" scheduling procedures), you would want to use this factor in determining when to schedule your classes.

    If you study best in the morning, for example, try to schedule as many classes as possible in the afternoons (or, at worst, late in the morning).

    If you study best in the evening, either schedule morning classes and leave your afternoons free for other activities, or schedule them in the afternoons so you can sleep later (and study later the night before).

7. Some of us get cranky if we try to do *anything* when we're hungry. If you study poorly when your stomach is growling, eat something!

8. Most of us grow up automatically studying alone. If we "study with a friend," there's often more horseplay than studying. But don't underestimate the positive effect studying with one or two friends—or even a larger study group—can have on your mastery of schoolwork and on your grades. (See the next section for more on study groups.)

9. Just because you perform best under pressure doesn't mean you should leave projects, papers and studying for tests until the last minute. It just means if you're well organized, but an unexpected project gets assigned or a surprise test announced, you won't panic.

    If you do *not* study well under pressure, it certainly doesn't mean you occasionally won't be required to.

The better organized you are, the easier it will be for you all the time, but especially when the unexpected arises.

10. As we've discussed, some of you (like me) will find it difficult to concentrate with*out* music or some sort of noise. Others couldn't sit in front of the TV and do *any*thing but breathe and eat.

    Many of you will fall in between—you can read and even take notes to music but need absolute quiet to study for a test or master particularly difficult concepts. If you don't know how you function best, now is the time to find out.

11. Back to organizing. The latter concept—starting and finishing one project before moving on to another—doesn't mean you can't at least sit down and outline an entire night's study plan before tackling each subject, one at a time. Setting up such a study schedule *is* advised. But it may mean you really *can't* move to another project while the one you're now working on is unfinished. Others of you may have no problem working on one project, switching to another when you get stuck or just need a break, then going back to the first.

12. There's nothing particularly wrong with taking a break whenever you feel you need to to keep yourself sharp and maximize your quality study time...as long as the breaks aren't every five minutes and don't last longer than the study periods! In general, though, try to increase your concentration through practice so that you can go at least an hour before getting up, stretching and having a drink or snack. Too many

projects will require at least that long to "get into" or organize, and you may find that breaking too frequently will require too much "review time" when you return to your desk.

Form your own study group

Find a small group of like-minded students—four to six seems to be an optimal number—and share notes, question each other, prepare for tests together. To be effective, obviously, the students you pick to be in your group should share all, or at least most, of your classes.

Search out students who are smarter than you, but not too much smarter. If they are on a level far beyond your own, you'll soon be left in the dust and be more discouraged than ever. On the other hand, if you choose students who are too far beneath your level, you may enjoy being the "Brain" of the bunch but miss the point of the group—the challenge of other minds to spur you on.

Study groups can be organized in a variety of ways. Each member of the group could be assigned primary responsibility for a single class, including preparing detailed notes from lectures and discussion groups. If supplementary reading is recommended but not required, that person could be responsible for doing all such reading and preparing detailed summaries.

(The extra work you will thus have to do in one class will be offset by the extra work others will be doing for you.)

Alternatively, everybody can be responsible for his or her own notes, but the group could act as an *ad hoc* discussion group, refining your understanding of key points, working on problems together, questioning each other, practicing for tests, etc.

Even if you find only one or two other students willing to work with you, such cooperation will be invaluable, especially in preparing for major exams.

Here's how to form your own study group and maximize its success:

- I suggest four students minimum, probably six maximum. You want to ensure everyone gets a chance to participate as much as they want while maximizing the collective knowledge and wisdom of the group.

   While group members needn't be best friends, they shouldn't be overtly hostile to one another, either. Seek diversity of experience, demand common dedication.

- Try to select students that are at least as smart, committed and serious as you. That will encourage you to keep up and challenge you a bit. Avoid a group in which you're the "star"—at least until you flame out during the first exam.

- There are a number of ways to organize, as we briefly discussed above. My suggestion is to assign each class to one student. That student must truly master that assigned class, doing, in addition to the regular assignments, of course, any or all additional reading (recommended by the professor or not) necessary to achieve that goal, taking outstanding notes, outlining the course (if the group decides that would be helpful), being available for questions about specific topics in the class and preparing various practice quizzes, midterms and finals, as needed, to help test the other students' mastery.

Needless to say, all of the other students still attend all classes, take their own notes, do their own reading and homework assignments. But the student assigned that class attempts to learn as much as the professor, to actually be the "substitute professor" of that class in the study group. (So if you have five classes, a five-person study group becomes the ideal.)

- Make meeting times and assignments formal and rigorous. Consider rigid rules of conduct. For example, miss two meetings, whatever the excuse, and you're out. Better to shake out the nonserious students early. You don't want anyone who is working as little as possible but hoping to take advantage of *your* hard work.

- However you organize, clearly decide—early—the exact requirements and assignments of each student. Again, you never want the feeling to emerge that one or two of you are trying to "ride the coattails" of the others.

Studying with small kids

So many more of you are going back to school while raising a family, I want to give you some ideas that will help you cope with the Charge of the Preschool Light Brigade:

Plan activities to keep the kids occupied. And out of your hair. The busier you are in school and/or at work, the more time your kids will want you when you *are* home. If you spend a little time with them, it may be easier for them to play alone, especially if you've planned ahead, creating projects *they* can work on while *you*'re working on your homework.

Make the kids part of your study routine. Kids love routine, so why not include them in yours? If 4 p.m. to 6 p.m. is always "Mommy's Study Time", the kids will soon get used to it, especially if you make spending other time with them a priority and if you take the time to give them something to do during your study hours. Explaining the importance of what you're doing—in a way that includes some ultimate benefit for *them*—will also motivate your children to become part of your "study team."

Use the television as a baby-sitter. While many of you will have a problem with this—one that I and my 5-year-old deal with weekly, if not daily—it may be the lesser of two evils. And you can certainly rent (or tape) enough quality shows so you don't have to worry about the little darlings are watching Ninja Turtles bash skulls in (or bashing skulls themselves on some video game system).

Plan your study accordingly. Unless you are right up there in the Perfect Parent Pantheon, all of these things will not keep your kids from interrupting you every now and then. While you can minimize such intrusions, it's virtually impossible to eliminate them entirely. So don't try—plan your schedule *assuming* there will be such interruptions. For one, that means taking more frequent breaks to spend five minutes with your kids. They'll be more likely to give you the 15 or 20 minutes at a time *you* need if they get periodic attention themselves. By default, *that* means avoiding projects that can only be done with an hour of massive concentration—you can only work in 15 or 20 minute bursts!

Find help. Spouses can occasionally take the kids out for dinner and a movie (and trust me, the kids will encourage you to study *more* if you do this!), relatives can baby-sit (at their homes) on a rotating basis, playmates can be invited over (allowing you to send your darling to their house the next day), you may be able to trade baby-sitting chores with other parents at school, and professional day-care may be available at your child's school or in someone's home for a couple of hours a day. Be creative in finding the help you need and scheduling accordingly.

My Ideal Study Environment

How I receive information best:

1. ❑ Orally ❑ Visually

In the classroom, I should:

2. ❑ Concentrate on taking notes ❑ Concentrate on
listening
3. ❑ Sit in front ❑ Sit in back ❑ Sit near window or door

Where I study best:

4. ❑ At home ❑ In the library ❑ Somewhere else:

_____

When I study best:

5. ❑ Every night; little on weekends ❑ Mainly on weekends
❑ Spread out over seven days
6. ❑ In the morning ❑ Evening ❑ Afternoon
7. ❑ Before dinner ❑ After dinner

How I study best:

8. ❑ Alone ❑ With a friend ❑ In a group
9. ❑ Under time pressure ❑ Before I know I have to
10. ❑ With music ❑ In front of TV ❑ In a quiet room
11. ❑ Organizing an entire night's studying before I start
❑ Tackling and completing one subject at a time

I need to take a break:

12. ❑ Every 30 minutes or so ❑ Every hour ❑ Every 2 hrs.
❑ Every ____ hours

Chapter Four

JUST MAKE YOURSELF TRY

Motivation is a key element in any time management program. Because without sufficient motivation and persistence, a schedule is just like a car without an engine: You won't enjoy its plush interior and crankin' stereo nearly as much if it won't take you where you want to go.

I'm on the outside, looking in

Motivators are either intrinsic or extrinsic. What's the difference? You sign up for a voice class. While the hours certainly apply to your graduating requirements, you attend class because you love singing. You look forward to completing each assignment, which usually involves singing and taping a solo to be played back for the class.

You also signed up for biology. You hate the thought of dissecting frogs, and you couldn't care less whether humans are exoskeletons, endoskeletons or hydroskeletons. But to fulfill your major, you have to take the class.

In the first scenario, you are motivated by *intrinsic* factors—you are taking the voice class for no other reason than that you truly enjoy it.

The second scenario is an example of *extrinsic* motivation. While you have no interest in biology, your reward for taking the class is external—by finishing it, you will be able to graduate.

Ways to motivate yourself

In order to increase the amount of intrinsic motivation you have for school, begin by taking stock of your personal interests. What areas of life intrigue you? Can you take classes in those subjects? Yes, school is primarily a path that leads you on to other things, but the more interested you are in the path, the more likely you'll reach your destination...and enjoy the journey, too.

Extrinsic motivation can help you make it through the boring or unpleasant tasks that are part of the process of reaching your goals. For example, you chose to major in journalism because you love to investigate and write about news events. You will undoubtedly find many of your classes fascinating.

Nevertheless, you may still struggle to maintain interest in your journalism law class. You may need some external motivation to help you do well in the course and reach the larger goals that you've set for yourself. Later in this chapter, we will discuss how to use artificial rewards to give yourself a boost if your motivation lags.

Manage Your Time

A vivid, visual image of your final goal can be a powerful motivating force. For example, one student thought about what his job as a computer programmer would be like whenever he needed a little help getting through difficult classes. Try imagining what a day in *your* life will be like five or ten years down the road. What will your career be like?

If you don't have the faintest clue, no *wonder* you're having a hard time motivating yourself to work toward that career as a final goal!

Your ultimate goal, while a valuable force, will not get you up every morning and keep you working for years. You need *intermediate* and *short-range* goals, too.

One student looking ahead to a career in medicine had "being a doctor" as her goal. But that was a target that was too vague and too long away—she ran out of steam long before reaching it. She should have looked for more immediate motivators—finishing a difficult course, graduating from college, getting into a good medical school.

Create a goal pyramid

One way to easily visualize all your goals—and their relation to each other—is to construct what I call a *goal pyramid*. Here's how to do it:

1. Centered at the top of a piece of paper, write down what you hope to ultimately gain from your education. This is your long-range goal and the pinnacle of your pyramid. Example: Become a successful advertising copywriter.

2. Below your long-range goal(s), list mid-range goals— milestones or steps that will lead you to your eventual target. For example, if your long-range goal were to

become an advertising copywriter, your mid-range goals might include getting into college, "acing" all your writing courses, completing all required courses and getting a summer internship at a major ad agency.

3. Below the mid-range goals, list as many short-range goals as you can—smaller steps which can be completed in a relatively short period of time. For example, if your long-range goal is to become a travel writer for a widely read magazine, your mid-range goal may be to earn a degree in journalism. Short-range goals may include writing a travel article to submit to the school paper, registering for magazine writing courses or getting an excellent grade in a related class.

The goals you set for yourself now should not be written in stone. Change your goal pyramid as you progress through school. You may eventually decide on a different career. Or your mid-range goals may change as you decide on a different path leading to the long-range goal. The short-range goals will change, often as a matter of course. They will be different even a week from now as your assignments and weekly tasks change.

The process of creating your own goal pyramid allows you to see *how* all those little daily and weekly steps you take can lead to your mid-range and long-term goals, and will thereby motivate you to work on your daily and weekly tasks with more energy and enthusiasm.

Make goal-setting a part of your life

The development of good study skills is the highway to your goals, whatever they are. And no matter how hard you have to work or how much adversity you have to overcome along the way, the journey will indeed be worth it.

How do you make setting goals a part of your life? Here are some hints I think will help:

1. *Be realistic about your goals*. Don't aim too high or too low and don't be particularly concerned when (not if) you have to make adjustments along the way.

2. *Be practical about your expectations*. An improved understanding of a subject you have little aptitude for is preferable to getting hopelessly bogged down if total mastery of the subject is just not in the cards.

3. *Beware the Goldilocks Conundrum*. Despite the previous two points, you can be *overly* realistic—too ready to sigh and give up just because something is just "too hot" or "too cold". There's a fine line between aiming too high and feeling miserable when you don't come close, aiming too low and never achieving your potential, and finding the path that's right for you.

4. *Concentrate on areas that offer the best chance for improvement.* Unexpected successes can do wonders for your confidence and might make it possible for you to achieve more than you thought in other areas.

5. *Monitor your achievements and keep resetting your goals.* Daily, weekly, monthly, yearly—ask yourself how you've done and where you'd like to go *now*.

Rewards can keep you going

The way you decide to use a reward system all depends on how much help you need getting motivated to study. As we've observed, tasks that are intrinsically interesting require little outside motivation. However, most schoolwork can be spurred along by the promise of little rewards along the way. If the task is especially tedious or difficult, make the rewards more frequent so that your motivation doesn't sag.

As a general rule, the size of the reward should match the difficulty of the task.

For an hour of reading, promise yourself a ten-minute walk. For completion of a rough draft for a big assignment, treat yourself to a movie.

For finishing the *final* draft, make sure it stars Mel Gibson or Julia Roberts and treat yourself to the largest bucket of popcorn!

Success begets success

Students often think they should be able to complete tasks out of sheer willpower. Many fear that if their will power is not strong enough, offering themselves rewards for something they should be doing anyway will further weaken their resolve.

Rewarding yourself can actually be a way of *strengthening* your self-discipline. If you consistently set up goals that are unreachable, all you are doing is practicing to fail. Practice makes perfect. Fail you will.

On the other hand, shooting to achieve smaller goals and rewarding yourself every time you reach them will build your list of *successes*. As you work on these study goals—and *reach* them—you'll begin to believe in yourself more and more, and your performance will continue to improve.

Remember, your purpose is not to suffer through school like a martyr. There's nothing wrong with making it as enjoyable as possible.

Are you Bugs Bunny or Elmer Fudd?

In trying to motivate yourself, do you tend to use the carrot or the stick? Positive and negative thoughts can both motivate.

The following are examples of *negative* thoughts that students have used to motivate themselves:

1. "If I don't get a good mark on this test, there goes my grade."
2. "If I don't finish this assignment, I'll have to miss the party."
3. "If I blow this college entrance exam, my future is shot."
4. "I'll be forced to go to summer school if I don't do well in this class."

Now here are some examples of *positive* thoughts that students have used to motivate themselves:

1. "For every hour of solid study, I get to listen to two songs on my new CD."
2. "If I get this assignment done early, I will be able to go skiing Friday."
3. "If I earn an 'A' in this class, I'll reward myself with a weekend at the beach."
4. "If I do well in these courses, my chances for grad school are excellent."

Which do you tend to use to motivate yourself, the carrot or the stick? If you're not sure, try the following exercise. Look at the next two pages. On the lines beneath the heading, "This Year's Successes," on page 77, list as many successes over the past year as you can think of. Examples might be getting a good grade on a term paper, getting a terrific grade for the semester, landing on the honor roll or dean's list, making a sports team, landing a part in a play or committing yourself to a fitness routine.

Then, on page 78, beneath the heading, "This Year's Failures," list as many failures as you can think of. All done? OK, now ask yourself, which list was the easiest to fill out? Look them over again. Which has the most items? Before you did this exercise, which items (positive or negative) did you tend to dwell on the most?

Chances are, many of you found it easier to list your failures than your successes. In fact, you may have discovered you didn't have enough *room* for all your failures, while you struggled to list even a few successes.

Turn your failures into successes

Well, I have something to say about success and failure. Failures are just as valuable experiences as successes—in fact, they may well be *more* valuable. What was one of the first lessons you learned in life? Not to touch a hot stove? Not to put your cat in the washing machine? Not to leave your talking doll out in the rain? And how did you discover these profound truths? Probably the hard way. Yet, you learned from these experiences, these "failures." Likewise, you can learn from *every* failure, and then turn it into a success.

Review your list of failures. Think about what you learned from each experience, then reword it so that it is a success story. For example, suppose one of your recent failures was that you turned in an English paper late, and, as a direct result of your lateness, received a lower grade.

Manage Your Time

What did this failure teach you? You learned that getting projects done on time is as important as doing them well. You realized that you had to learn to manage your time better, so you picked up this book and you've committed yourself to implementing a good time management system. You're now taking control of your life.

Congratulations!

You've just turned your failure into a success story!

There is no rule against using the stick to motivate yourself. But learn to turn your failures into successes—this will keep your attitude positive and keep the wind in your sails. Focusing on the positive helps you feel good about yourself and provides excitement to keep you motivated.

This Year's Successes

This Year's Failures

_____

_____

_____

_____

_____

_____

_____

_____

_____

_____

_____

_____

_____

_____

_____

_____

_____

_____

_____

_____

_____

_____

_____

_____

_____

_____

_____

_____

Chapter Five

GET THE BIG PICTURE

Now you're ready to plan!

We'll begin by developing a time management plan for an entire term...before it begins, of course.

This term plan will allow you to keep your sights on the "big picture."

To see the forest, even when you're in the midst of the trees...and a majority of them are oversized redwoods.

By being able to take in your entire term—every major assignment, every test, every paper, every appointment—you will be less likely to get caught up spending more time on a lower-priority class, just because it requires regularly scheduled reports, while falling behind in a more important one, which only requires reading.

And when you can actually *see* you have a test in accounting the same week your zoology project is due, you can plan ahead and finish the project early. If you decide —for whatever reason—not to do so, at least you won't be caught by surprise when crunch time comes.

Start planning early

For your long-term planning to be effective, however, you must start early. Students who fail to plan *before* the school term begins often find themselves wasting time filling in their schedule one event at a time during the term. They may also find themselves feeling disorganized throughout the term. Starting early, on the other hand, increases your ability to follow a systematic plan of attack.

All college students—and some high school students—are able to pick and choose courses according to their own schedules, likes, dislikes, goals, etc. The headiness of such freedom should be tempered with the common-sense approach you're trying to develop through reading this book. Here are a few hints to help you along:

- Whenever possible, consider each professor's reputation as you decide whether to select a particular course (especially if it is an overview or introductory course that is offered in two or three sessions). Word soon gets around as to which professor's lectures are stimulating and rewarding—an environment in which learning is a joy, even if it isn't a subject you like!

- Attempt to select classes so that your schedule is balanced on a weekly and even a daily basis, though this will not always be possible or advisable. (Don't change your major just to fit your schedule!) Try to leave an open hour or half-hour between classes—it's ideal for review, post-class note-taking, quick trips to the library, etc.

- Try to alternate challenging classes with those that come more easily to you. Studying is a process of positive reinforcement. You'll need encouragement along the way.

- Avoid late-evening or early-morning classes, especially if such scheduling provides you with large gaps of "down time."

- Set a personal study pace and follow it. Place yourself on a study diet, the key rule of which is: *Don't over-eat.*

It's all routine, Mr. Watson

You can't race off to your ultimate goal until you figure out where *your* starting line is. So the first step to overhaul your current routine is to *identify* that routine, in detail. My suggestion is to chart, in 15-minute increments, how you spend every minute of every day *right now*. While a day or two might be sufficient for some of you, I recommend you chart your activities for an entire week, including the weekend.

This is especially important if, like many people, you have huge pockets of time that seemingly disappear, but, in reality are devoted to things like "resting" after you wake up, putting on makeup or shaving, reading the paper, waiting for transportation or driving to and from school or work. Could you use an extra hour or two a day, either for studying or for fun? Make better use of such "dead" time and you find all the time you need.

Manage Your Time

For example, learn how to do multiple tasks at the same time. Listen to a book on tape while you're working around the house; practice vocabulary or math drills while you're driving; have your kids, parents or roommates quiz you for an upcoming test while you're doing dishes, vacuuming or dusting; *always* carry your calendar, notebook(s), pens and a textbook with you—you can get a phenomenal amount of reading or studying done while in line at the bank, in the library, at the supermarket or on a bus or train.

The more ready you are to transform "dead" time into study time, the more ways you'll invent for yourself.

Strategy Tip: Identify those items on your daily calendar, whatever their priority, that can be completed in 15 minutes or less. These are the ideal tasks to tackle at the laundromat, while waiting for a book to wind its way to your study cubicle or while standing in line anywhere.

One of the inherent advantages of a strictly observed schedule is that it saves time just by "being"—eliminating all that time so many of us waste just sitting down wondering what we should do next! (Not to mention trying to find the materials we need, deciding where we're going to study that night, how long, with whom, etc., etc., etc.) The more time management becomes a *habit*, the more *automatic* such decisions become, and the less time you waste making them.

The other huge advantage, of course, is the discipline such a strict schedule demands. Discipline is a wonderful commodity in that, as far as I've found, the more you're able to discipline *any* single aspect of your life, the easier it is to discipline all others. Just ask any writer who's confronted a blank sheet of paper and stared...for hours..."blocked" by unseen forces. Many will tell you the only way to break free is to continue sitting, day after day, trying again and again, no matter how difficult. You don't think *that* takes discipline?

Collect what you need

As you begin your planning session, make sure you have all of the information and materials you need to make a quality plan. Gather your class syllabuses; work schedule; dates of important family events, vacations or trips, other personal commitments (doctor appointments, birthday parties, etc.); and a calendar of any extracurricular events in which you plan to participate.

Keeping track of your day-to-day activities—classes, appointments, regular daily homework assignments and daily or weekly quizzes—will be dealt with in the next chapter. For now, I want to talk about those projects—studying for midterm and final exams, term papers, theses, etc.—that require completion over a long period of time. Weeks. Maybe even months.

Creating your Project Board

There are two excellent tools you can use for your long-term planning. The first is a Project Board, which you can put on any blank wall or right above your desk.

It's not necessary for you to construct your own Project Board, though it is certainly the least expensive alternative. There are ready-made charts for professionals available in a variety of formats, including magnetic and erasable. (Yes, you're learning something that you can use throughout your life: Professionals call Project Boards flow charts.) Your local art supply, stationery or bookstore may have a selection of such items. Otherwise, you can certainly copy the format of the one I've reproduced on pages 84 and 85.

How does the Project Board work? As you can see, it is just a variation on a calendar. I have set it up vertically—the months

Sample Projects Board

MONTH/WEEK		PROJECT: STUDENT CORPORATION
1st MONTH	Week 1	Initial group meeting: Discuss overall assignment and possible products or services—bring list of three each to meeting (1 hour)
	Week 2	Finalize product or service; finalize organization of group and longterm responsibilities of each subgroup. (3)
	Week 3	Subgroup planning and short-term assignments (2)
	Week 4	Work on individual assignment from subgroup (?)
2nd MONTH	Week 1	Work on individual assignment from subgroup (?)
	Week 2	Work on individual assignment from subgroup (?)
	Week 3	Integrate individual assignment with rest of subgroup (?)
	Week 4	Meet with entire group to integrate plans (?)
3rd MONTH	Week 1	Finalize all-group plan; draft initial report (?)
	Week 2	Type and proof final report (?)
	Week 3	
	Week 4	
	DUE DATE	3RD MONTH/end of Week 2

PROJECT: DANTE TERM PAPER	REVIEW/EXAM SCHEDULE
Finalize topic (1 hour)	Review prior month's History notes (3)
Initial library research (2) General outline (1)	Review prior month's English notes (2)
Detailed library research (3)	Review prior month's Science notes (4)
Detailed library research (3)	Review prior month's Math notes (4)
Detailed library research (3)	Review 1st MONTH History notes (3)
Detailed outline (1)	Review 1st MONTH English notes (2)
First draft (4), Additional research (2)	Review 1st MONTH Science notes (4)
	Review 1st MONTH Math notes (4)
Second draft, spellcheck, proof (10)	2nd MONTH History notes (3)
Independent proof (1)	2nd MONTH English notes (2)
	2nd MONTH Science notes (4)
Type final draft and proof (4)	2nd MONTH Math notes (4)
end of 3RD MONTH	end of 3RD MONTH

running down the left-hand side, the projects across the top. You can certainly switch and have the dates across the top and the projects running vertically (in fact, that's the way a lot of the ready-made ones come). It all depends on what space you have on your wall.

The more time you have to complete a project, the easier it is to procrastinate about dealing with it, even to putting off identifying the steps and working them into your regular schedule. If you find yourself leaving such long-term projects to the last week, schedule the projects furthest away—the term paper due in three months, the oral exam 10 weeks from now—*first*. Then, trick yourself—schedule the completion date at least seven days prior to the actual turn-in date, giving yourself a one-week cushion for life's inevitable surprises. (Just try to forget you've used this trick. Otherwise, you'll be like the perennial latecomer who set his watch 15 minutes fast in an effort to finally get somewhere on time. Except that he always reminded himself to add 15 minutes to the time on his wrist, defeating the whole purpose.)

Using your Project Board

In the case of each project, there is a key preparatory step before you can use the chart: You have to break down each general assignment into its component parts, the specific tasks involved in any large project. For example, presuming you have been assigned a paper on Dante for your English class, we can identify the steps necessary to complete it as follows:

1. Finalize topic
2. Initial library research
3. Prepare general outline

4. Detailed library research
5. Prepare detailed outline
6. Write first draft
7. Write second draft
8. Check spelling and proofread
9. Get someone else to proofread
10. Type final draft
11. Proofread again
12. Turn it in!

Next to each specific task, we have estimated the time we would expect to spend on it. (For more information about the steps required to write a winning term paper, I urge you to get a copy of the new second edition of *Write Papers,* another of the seven books in my **HOW TO STUDY** *Program.*)

The second project involves working on a team with other students from your entrepreneurship class to create a hypo-thetical student business. While the particular elements are different, you'll notice that the concept of breaking the project down into separate and manageable steps and allocating time for each of them doesn't change.

However, because time allocation in later steps depends on what assignments you're given by the group, we have had to temporarily place question marks next to some of them. As the details of this project become clearer and specific assignments are made, your Project Board should be changed to reflect both more details and the specific time required for each step.

You should also include on your Project Board time for studying for all your final exams. Cramming for tests doesn't work very well in the short term and doesn't work at all over the long term, so take my advice and made it a habit to review your class notes on each subject on a *weekly or monthly* basis. Let's presume you agree with me and have decided that every Sunday morning is "review time" and allocated one Sunday a month to review the previous month's work in each subject. We've entered this time on our Board, as well.

As a result of this plan, you'll notice there is little time allocated to "last-minute" cramming or even studying for a specific final the week before it is given; just a couple of hours to go over any details you're still a little unsure of or to spend on areas you think will be on the test. While others are burning the midnight oil in the library the night before each exam, you're getting a good night's sleep and will enter the tests refreshed, relaxed and confident. Seems like a better plan to me.

As a byproduct of this study schedule, by the way, you will find that salient facts and ideas will remain with you long after anybody is testing you on them.

Now that you have your Project Board, what do you do with it? Keep adding any and all other important projects throughout the term and continue to revise it according to actual time spent as opposed to time allocated. Getting into this habit will make you more aware of how much time to allocate to future projects and make sure that the more you do so, the more accurate your estimates will be.

Using a Term-Planning Calendar

The Term-Planning Calendar, an example of which is shown on pages 90 and 91, can be used in concert with or in place of the Project Board.

To use it with the Project Board, start by transferring all the information from the Project Board to your Term Planning Calendar. Then *add* your weekly class schedule, work schedule, family celebrations, vacations and trips, club meetings and extracurricular activities. *Everything.* The idea is to make sure your Calendar has *all* your scheduling information, while your Project Board contains just the briefest summary that you can ingest in a glance. (Note: The format of the calendar I've reproduced, while helpful as an illustration, is probably too small for your use, especially if you follow my advice and write *everything* down, from grocery lists to class assignments. Get the size calendar in the format that works best for you and your schedule.)

Leave your Project Board on your wall at home; carry your Term Planning Calendar with you. Whenever new projects, appointments, meetings, etc. are scheduled, add them immediately to your Calendar. Then transfer the steps involving major projects to your Project Board.

To use it in place of the Project Board, just don't make a Project Board. Put all the information—including the steps of all your projects and the approximate time you expect each to take—right on the Calendar.

It's up to you which way to go. Personally, I prefer using *both*, for one simple reason: I like being able to look at the wall and see the entire term *at a glance.* I find it much easier to see how everything "fits" together this way than by trying to "glance" at a dozen different weekly calendars or even three monthly ones.

I also find it difficult to easily see which steps go with which projects without studying the calendar (although I admit color-coding would solve this problem), whereas the very set-up of the Project Board makes such information easy to glean.

High school students may find it quite easy to use only the Term Planning Calendar, as they are usually not subject to quite as many long-term projects as college or graduate students. But

Manage Your Time

Month	Mon	Tue	Wed	Thu	Fri	Sat	Sun
Feb →	18	19	20	21	22	23	24
← March	25	26	27 conference 4-5	28	1	2	3
	4	5	6	7	8 Afternoon: A.A.P. meeting	9	10
	11 Sociology Presentation	12	13 Math: Ch.1-3	14	15	16	17 Trip Home
→	18	19	20 Math: Ch 4	21	22	23	24

Month	Mon	Tue	Wed	Thu	Fri	Sat	Sun
	25	26	27 Math: Ch.5	28	29	30	31
April	1	2	3 No Math Due	4	5	6 Trip to Jim & Dana's	7
	8	9	10 Math: Ch. 6 – 8	11	12 Sociology Paper due!	13	14
	15 Biology Lab Journal Due!!	16 Last day of class	17	18	19	20 Biology Final 3:00	21
	22 Math Final 2:00	23	24	25	26 ☺	27	28

← CAMPING !!! →

once you're in college, especially if you have more than an average number of papers, reports, projects, etc., you'll find the Project Board a very helpful extra tool.

And, yes, I realize it seems a "waste of time" to have to write all these details on both a Project Board and Term Planning Calendar. But I think you'll find the time you *save* more than makes up for the supposed inconvenience.

Chapter Six

ADD THE DETAILED BRUSH STROKES

Your Project Board now lists the major papers, projects and exams for an entire term. If you've done it the way I do, this Board is now taking up a wall in your room. And you've also filled out a Term Planning Calendar, filling in not just the details on your Project Board, but other key appointments, assignments and due dates.

It's time to become even more organized. The Project Board and Term Planning Calendar have given you a good start by helping you schedule the entire term. Now it's time to learn about the tools that will help you organize your days and weeks.

For any time management system to work, it has to be used continually. Before you go on, make an appointment with yourself for the end of the week—Sunday night is perfect—to sit down and plan for the following week. You don't have to spend a *lot* of time—a half hour is probably all it will take to review your commitments for the week and schedule the necessary study time.

Despite its brevity, this may just be the best time you spend all week, because you will reap the benefits of it throughout the week and beyond!

Step 1: Make your "To Do" list

First, you must identify everything you need to do this week. Look at your Project Board and/or Planning Calendar to determine what tasks need to be completed this week for all your major school projects. Add any other tasks that must be done—from sending off a birthday present to your sister to attending your monthly volunteer meeting to completing home-work that may have just been assigned.

Once you have created your list, you can move on to the next step, putting your tasks in order of importance.

Step 2: Prioritize your tasks

When you sit down to study without a plan, you just dive into the first project that comes to mind. The problem with this approach has been discussed earlier: There is no guarantee that the first thing that comes to mind will be the most important. The point of the weekly Priority Task Sheet is to help you arrange your tasks *in order of importance.* That way, even if you find yourself without enough time for *everything,* you can at least finish the most important assignments.

First, ask yourself this question, "If I only got a few things done this week, what would I want them to be?" Mark these high-priority tasks with an "H." After you have identified the "urgent" items, consider those tasks that are least important,—items that could wait until the following week to be done, if necessary. (This may include tasks you consider very important but that don't have to be completed *this week.*) These are low-priority items, at least for this week—you should mark them with an "L."

All the other items fit somewhere between the critical tasks and the low-priority ones. Review the remaining items. If you're sure none of them are either "H" or "L", mark them with an "M", for middle priority.

Strategy Tip: If you push aside the same low-priority item day after day, week after week, at some point you should just stop and decide whether it's something you need to do at all! This is a strategic way to make a task or problem "disappear." In the business world, some managers purposefully avoid confronting a number of problems, waiting to see which will simply solve themselves through benign neglect. If it works in business, it can work for you in school.

A completed Priority Task Sheet is on page 98. A blank form you can photocopy is on page 123.

Step 3: Fill in your Daily Schedule

Before you start adding papers, projects, homework, study time, etc., to your calendar, fill in the "givens"—the time you need to sleep, eat, work, attend class. Even if your current routine consists of meals on the run and sleep wherever you find it, build the assumption *right into your schedule* that you are going to get eight hours of sleep and three decent meals a day. You may surprise yourself and find that there is still enough time to do everything you need. (Though all of us probably know someone who sleeps three hours a night, eats nothing but junk and still finds a way to get straight As, most experts would contend that regular, healthy eating and a decent sleep schedule are key attributes to any successful study system.)

Now you're ready to transfer the items on your Priority Task Sheet to your Daily Schedule forms. (See page 99 for a sample completed Daily Schedule, page 124 for a blank form you can photocopy.)

Put in the "H" items first, followed by the "M" items. Then, fit in as many of the "L" items that you still have room for. By following this procedure, you'll make sure you devote the amount of time needed for your most important priorities. You can schedule your most productive study time for your most important tasks, and plug in your lower priorities as they fit.

Your three-hour block of free time Wednesday afternoon? Schedule your "H"-priority research-gathering, and plan to start that psychology assignment, an "L" priority, between lunch and your 2 p.m. class Thursday.

Other considerations

Besides the importance of the task and the available time you have to complete it, other factors will determine how you fit your Daily Schedules together. Some factors will be beyond your control—work schedules, appointments with professors, counselors, doctors. But there are plenty of factors you *do* control and should consider as you put together your Daily Schedules each week.

Schedule enough time for each task—time to "warm up" and get the task accomplished, but, particularly when working on long-term projects, not so much time that you "burn out." Every individual is different, but most students study best for blocks of one and a half to three hours, depending on the subject. You might find history fascinating and be able to read on the subject for hours. Calculus, on the other hand, may be a subject you handle best in "small bites," a half-hour to an hour at a time.

Don't overdo it. Plan your study time in blocks, breaking up work time with short leisure activities. (It's helpful to add these to your schedule as well.) For example, you've set aside three hours on Wednesday afternoon for that research assignment: Schedule a 15-minute walk to the ice cream shop somewhere in the middle of that study block. You'll find that these breaks help you think more clearly and creatively when you get back to studying.

Even if you tend to like longer blocks of study time, be careful about scheduling study "marathons"—a six- or eight-hour stretch rather than a series of two-hour sessions. The longer the period you schedule, the more likely you'll have to fight the demons of procrastination. Convincing yourself that you are really studying your heart out, you'll also find it easier to justify time-wasting distractions, scheduling longer breaks, and, before long, quitting before you should.

Use your Daily Schedule *daily*

Each night (or in the morning before the day begins) look at your schedule for the upcoming day. How much free time is there? Are there "surprise" tasks that are *not* on your schedule but need to be? Are there conflicts you were unaware of at the beginning of the week?

If you plan well at the beginning of the week, this shouldn't happen often. But it invariably does. Just as often you'll dicover a class is canceled or a meeting postponed, which leaves you with a schedule change. By checking your Daily Schedule *daily—either the night before or the first thing in the morning*—you'll be able to respond to these changes.

Manage Your Time

Priority Rating	Scheduled?	**Priority Tasks This Week** Week of **3/28** through **4/3**
		Sociology Paper
H		— Library Search
M		— Outline
L		— Rough Draft
		Math Assignments
H		— Ch. 4
M		— Ch. 5
M		— Study for test

Daily Schedule

date: **3/30**

Assignments Due

Bio. Lab work.
Math, Ch. 4

To Do/Errands

Call Erin — 871-4031
Books to library
☐ Bank
☐ Groceries
Drop by Jim's

Homework

1) Math Ch.5 1-9
2) Sociology paper (rough draft)

Schedule

5	
6	
7	
8	
9	Biology
10	Sociology
11	
12	Lunch w/ Kim
1	read:
2	ch.5 (soc.)
3	Math class
4	TRAVEL
5	
6	Math homework
7	work on paper
8	
9	
10	
11	
12	

How do you know whether to enter an assignment on your Daily Schedule or put it on the Project Board first?

If it's a simple task *and* if it will definitely be accomplished within a week—read pages 59-78, study for quiz, meet to discuss Cheerleader tryouts with faculty—put it on the appropriate Daily Schedule Sheet(s).

If, however, it's a task that is complicated—requiring further breakdown into specific steps—and/or one that will require more than a week to complete, it should be 'flow charted' on your Project Board. *Then* the individual steps should be added to your Daily Schedules. (I personally like to plan everything out the night before. It's a fantastic feeling to wake up and start the day completely organized.)

You'll benefit every day

Once you start using your Project Board, Term Planning Calendar, Priority Task Sheets and Daily Schedules, you will reap the benefits every day. Throughout the day, you can simply follow your daily schedule.

Anything—even school—seems less overwhelming when you have it broken into "bite-size" pieces and you already know the flavor.

You no longer worry about when you'll get that paper done—you've already planned for it.

You'll accomplish it *all*—one step at a time.

As you get used to managing your time—planning your months, your weeks and even your days—you'll quickly discover that you seem to have more time than you ever had before.

Chapter Seven

HELP! TIPS, TIPS AND MORE TIPS

In this book, you've learned a simple, manageable system for getting more done in the amount of time you have available. It is a system geared exactly for people like *you*—students whose school schedules demand a big chunk of time, yet who have a myriad of other commitments, activities and responsibilities pulling you in other directions.

Your time management plan should be simple. Why commit to another complicated project that demands your time and mental energies? Yet, no matter how basic and easy to use your time management program may be, this doesn't guarantee that you won't be plagued with a time-crunch problem from time to time.

As you try to implement the suggested time management skills in your life, you are bound to have some glitches. It is impossible to completely avoid these study roadblocks, no matter what you do. It's worthwhile to learn some problem-solving skills so they don't stop your progress completely.

Hitting the "wall"

If you run into a "wall" on your path to time management success, the best solution is to find creative ways to get *around* it, rather than trying to crash your way *through* it.

If you were trying to lose weight, for example, there are a number of different approaches you could take:

You could try to alter your *behavior*—eat less, exercise more.

Or change your *attitude* toward eating, maybe stop using food as a reward.

Or transform your *environment*, keeping the refrigerator stocked with only healthy fruits and veggies...and moving your study area from the kitchen to the bedroom!

Most likely, your weight loss will come about from a *combination* of changes in all three areas.

Here are several examples of creative and multidimensional approaches to solving typical time management problems:

Time flies when you're having fun...

...And sometimes even when you're *not*. No matter how hard you try to stick to your schedule, you find that your assignments always take a lot longer than you had planned. You schedule an hour to do your economics homework, and it takes you twice that long. You plan an afternoon at the library for research, and it's closing time before you're ready to leave. It seems like you spend all your time studying—and you're *still* not getting it done.

Solutions: It's time for an attitude check. Are you being too much of a perfectionist? Is it taking you so long to read because you're trying to memorize every word? Make sure your expectations for yourself are realistic. And don't exaggerate the importance of lower-priority assignments.

Consider altering your behavior—with a little help from an alarm clock. If you've planned an hour for your reading assignment, set the clock to go off when you should have completed it. Then, *stop reading.* And go on to the next assignment. If you're not done, reassure yourself that you can go back to it later. You'll probably become conditioned to complete your assignments more quickly, and you won't run the risk of leaving your other, perhaps more important, work unfinished.

"I'm allergic to my desk"

There's nothing wrong with your study area. It's in a quiet corner of the house with few distractions. All your materials are nearby, and the area is well-lit and well-ventilated. But...every time you sit down to study, you find yourself coming up with *any* excuse to leave. Unable to focus on any assignment, your mind would be wandering out the window if there were one in front of you.

Solution: It can happen. You set up the ideal study area, follow your time management system and stick to your schedule religiously. Your intentions are good. But, for some reason, it just doesn't work. Bad vibes, maybe.

What can you do?

Change your environment!

Just as you can condition yourself to study, you can also condition yourself *not* to study in a particular area. Stick to your schedule, but try another area—another floor in the library, even a place that may not seem to be as conducive to quiet study. Maybe you're one of those people who needs a little music in the background to concentrate.

If changing your environment doesn't help, consider your behavior. Are you trying to study at a time of day when you have too much pent-up energy? Maybe switching your study time earlier or later would help. Try taking a brisk walk or exercising before you begin studying.

Think about other behavior: Have you had several cups of coffee (or cans of soda) prior to your study period? Caffeine overdose—or too much sugar *and* caffeine—could make it very difficult to concentrate.

A conspiracy to keep you from studying

Friends and family call when you're studying because they know that's the best time to reach you at home. Or you're interrupted by phone calls for family members or roommates. Worse yet are the calls from people taking surveys, asking for donations, or trying to sell you.

Solutions: A ringing phone is virtually impossible to ignore. Even if you're determined not to pick it up, it still demands your attention. A phone-answering machine will eliminate your getting roped into lengthy conversations, but your train of thought will still be interrupted.

There are two environment-altering solutions: Unplug the phone while you're studying. Or remove yourself from within hearing distance—go to the library.

A little help from your "friends"

Your roommate, whose study hours differ from yours, always seems to want to spend "quality bonding time" in the middle of your heavy-duty reading assignments.

Solutions: It's not rude to refuse to talk to someone while you're studying. But it often feels like that, and I'd rather feel guilty about not studying than being rude to a friend. A favorite tip from human-relations specialists is to respond in a positive but diverting way—e.g., "It sounds like this is important to you. I really want to hear more. Can we talk in an hour when I'm done with this, so I can concentrate more on your problem?" (Granted, your roommate would look at you as if you were crazy if you talked like this. Put it in your own words—it's the attitude that's important.)

Another solution might be to put up a "Do Not Disturb" sign, indicating the time you will be available to talk. The visual signal helps remind others that you're busy before they unintentionally interrupt you with small talk.

You can't count on anyone

You painstakingly plan your schedule each week, religiously keeping track of each appointment, assignment and commitment you have. Unfortunately, others don't seem to have the same sense of responsibility you do. Your friends cancel social engagements, you arrive on time for a meeting and no one else in the group shows up, even your teacher postpones the pre-test study session.

Solution: Yes, its time for another attitude adjustment. Welcome to the real world!

First of all, there's nothing you can do when someone else cancels or postpones a scheduled appointment. But if you remember, in the very first chapter of this book, I said that fanaticism is not an element of a good time management program.

Occasional—and sometimes more than occasional—cancellations, postponements or reschedulings should *not* ruin your schedule.

Try looking at such last-minute changes as *opportunities.* Your doctor canceled your appointment? That means a free hour to get ahead in calculus, read your history, work out at the health center—or just do nothing!

A special note for commuters

If you live at home (as opposed to being housed on campus), there are some special pressures with which you need to be ready to contend:

- Travel time. Your commute to school will probably be longer than a roll out of bed and walk to class. It will certainly require more wakefulness, even if you just have to stumble to a subway or bus (but especially if you have to drive!). You'll also have travel time problems if you need to use the library after you've returned home or, for that matter, need to return to the campus for any reason. It's especially important *you* minimize your travel time, planning enough to maximize your use of the campus facilities without scheduling a trip home in between.
- While nobody likes walking to class in rain, sleet or snow, it is invariably easier to walk a few tree-lined blocks than drive a few miles in inclement weather. Take weather problems into account when scheduling your commute.
- The very act of living at home—whether as a child or one "married with children"—brings with it responsibilities to others you could minimize living in a dorm. Be ready to allocate time to these responsibilities and include them in your study schedule. They're as inevitable if you live at home as meat loaf on Tuesdays.

Old habits die hard

As you begin to implement your own system of time management, you may need to rid yourself of some old habits:

1. *Don't make your schedule overly vague.* For example, when Kirsten planned out her day, she simply wrote "study" in the blank spaces on her schedule. Although she had good intentions, she had difficulty actually *studying*. Often she found that the book she needed was still at home, or she had to ask someone about the details of the assignment she needed to finish.

    When you're scheduling your time, be specific about which tasks you plan to do, and when you plan to do them. When Kirsten wrote "read 15 pages in History text" rather than "study" in her calendar, she did not forget her book.

2. *Don't delay your planning.* It's easy to convince yourself that you will plan the details of a particular task when the time comes. You may tell yourself, "I'll just leave my schedule blank and plan the afternoon right after I get out of Biology." But that way it's much too easy to forget your homework when your friends invite you to go to the park or out for a snack.

3. *Write* everything *down.* All of the tools we've discussed and the various other hints should get you into the habit of writing things down. Not having to remember all these items will free up space in your brain for the things you need to concentrate on or *do* have to remember. As a general rule, write down the so-called little things and you'll avoid data overload and clutter.

4. *Learn to manage distractions.* As a time management axiom puts it, "Don't respond to the urgent and forget the important." It's easy to become distracted when the phone rings, your baby brother chooses to trash your room or you realize your favorite TV show is coming on. But don't just drop your books and run off. Take a few seconds to make sure you have reached a logical stopping point. If you haven't, get back to work. If you have, jot down a note to yourself of exactly where you left off and/or anything you want to remember after your break. Then you can enjoy your break without anxiety.

5. *Don't "shotgun" plan.* Even if you haven't been following a systematic time management approach, you may have had some way of keeping important dates and events in mind. Some students use what might be called the "shotgun" approach—writing down assignments, dates and times on whatever paper is available. They wind up with so many slips of paper in so many places, their planning attempts are virtually worthless.

Darren, for example, kept numerous calendars and schedules. In his class notes he wrote down when his assignments were due. He had a calendar in his room with all the holidays marked. He kept his school catalog because it had a list of all important school deadlines and the dates of finals. He had another calendar of events which was provided by his church group. As you can imagine, he rarely had all of his records with him at once.

Record all upcoming events and tasks on your Project Board and/or Term Planning Calendar. And always have your calendar with you so you can refer to it when you are planning a specific week or day or need to add an appointment or assignment to it.

6. *Don't "overschedule."* As you begin to follow a time management program, you may find yourself trying to schedule too *much* of your time. Once you get the "effectiveness bug" and become aware of how much you can accomplish, it might be tempting to squeeze more and more into your life.

7. *Be realistic and honest with yourself* when determining those things that require more effort, those that come easier to you. Chances are you can't complete the outline for your term paper, study three chapters of Biology and do your French assignment in the two hours you have between class and work. Schedule enough time to get each assignment done. Whenever possible, schedule pleasurable activities *after* study time, not before. They will then act as incentives, not distractions.

8. *Remember that time is relative.* Car trips take longer if you have to schedule frequent stops for gas, food, necessities, etc., longer still if you start out during rush hour. Likewise, libraries are more crowded at certain times of the day or year, which will effect how fast you can get books you need, etc. So take the time of day into account.

And if your schedule involves working with others, you need to take *their* sense of time into account—you may find you have to schedule "waiting time" for a chronically-late friend...and always bring a book along.

9. *Be prepared.* As assignments are entered on your calendar, make sure you also enter items needed—texts,

other books you have to buy, borrow or get from the library, special materials, etc. There's nothing worse than sitting down to do that assignment you've put off until the last minute—you may not have perfected your time management system yet-and realizing that though *you're* finally ready to get to work, your supplies *aren't*...and at 10 p.m., you don't have a lot of options!

10. *Be realistic.* Plan according to *your* schedule, *your* goals and *your* aptitudes, not some ephemeral "standard." Allocate the time you expect a project to take *you*, not the time it might take someone else, how long your teacher tells you it should take, etc. There will be tasks you accomplish far faster than anyone else, others that take you much longer.

11. *Be flexible, monitor and adjust.* No calendar is an island. Any new assignment will affect whatever you've already scheduled. If you have a reasonably light schedule when a new assignment suddenly appears, it can just be plugged right into your calendar and finished as scheduled. But if you've already planned virtually every hour for the next two weeks, *any* addition may force you to change a whole day's plan. Be flexible and be ready. It'll happen.

And remember that no plan of action is foolproof, so monitor your progress at reasonable periods and make changes where necessary. This is *your* study regimen-you conceived it, you can change it.

12. *Look for more time savings.* If you find that you are consistently allotting more time than necessary to a specific chore—giving yourself one hour to review your English notes every Sunday but always finishing

in 45 minutes or less—change your future schedule accordingly. You may use the extra 15 minutes for a task that consistently takes *longer* than you've anticipated or, if such doesn't exist, quit 15 minutes early.

13. *Accomplish one task before going on to the next one*—don't skip around. If you ever stuffed envelopes for a political candidate, for example, you've probably already learned that it is far quicker and easier to sign 100 letters, then stuff them into envelopes, then seal and stamp them than to sign, stuff, seal and stamp one letter at a time.

14. *Do your least favorite chores* (study assignments, projects, whatever) first—you'll feel better having gotten them out of the way! And plan how to accomplish them as meticulously as possible. That will get rid of them even faster.

15. *Try anything that works.* You may decide that color coding your calendar—red for assignments that must be accomplished that week, blue for steps in longer-term projects (which give you more flexibility), yellow for personal time and appointments, green for classes, etc.—makes it easier for you to tell at a glance what you need to do and when you need to do it.

Or that you require a day-to-day calendar to carry with you, but a duplicate one on the wall at home.

Once you've gotten used to your class schedule, you may decide to eliminate class times from your calendar and make it less complicated.

16. *Adapt these tools to your own use.* Try anything you think may work—use it if it does, discard it if it doesn't.

Manage Your Time

There are thinkers and there are doers.

And there are those who think a lot about doing.

Organizing your life requires you to actually *use* the Project Board, Term Calendar, Priority Task Sheets and Daily Schedules we've discussed, not just waste more time "planning" instead of studying!

Planning is an ongoing learning process. Dive in and plan for your upcoming school term. Or, if you're in the middle of a term now, plan the remainder of it right now. As you use your plan in the upcoming weeks and months, you will come up with new ideas for improving your time management system in the future, and in tailoring it to your own needs.

As you get used to managing your time, planning ahead as well as planning your week and even your days, you'll quickly discover that you seem to have more time than ever before.

I hope you use it wisely and well!

Chapter Eight

IT'S TIME TO DEAL WITH ADD

We both fear and pity kids on illegal drugs. But we also must face and deal with what's happening to the 3 million-plus who are on a *legal* drug—Ritalin, the prescribed drug of choice for kids diagnosed with Attention Deficit Disorder (ADD), hyperactivity or the combination of the two (ADHD).

I could write a book on ADD, which seems to be the "diagnosis of choice" for school kids these days. Luckily, I don't have to. Thom Hartmann has already written an excellent one— *Attention Deficit Disorder: A Different Perception*—from which I have freely and liberally borrowed (with his permission) for this chapter.

I'm going to leave others to debate whether ADD actually exists as a clearly definable illness, whether it's the "catchall" diagnosis of lazy doctors, whether teachers are labeling kids as

ADD to avoid taking responsibility for the students' poor learning skills, whether Ritalin is a miracle drug or one that is medicating creative kids into a conforming stupor.

All of these positions *have* been asserted, and, as hundreds of new kids are medicated every day, the debate about ADD is only likely to continue...and heat up.

That is not my concern in this book.

What I want to deal with here is the reality that many kids, however they're labeled, have severe problems in dealing with school as it usually exists. And to give them the advice they need—especially regarding note-taking—to contend with the symptoms that have acquired the label "ADD".

Some definitions, please

Just what is ADD? It's probably easiest to describe as a person's difficulty focusing on a simple thing for any significant period of time. People with ADD are described as easily distracted, impatient, impulsive and often seeking immediate gratitude. They often have poor listening skills and have trouble doing "boring" jobs (like sitting quietly in class or, as adults, balancing a checkbook). "Disorganized" and "messy" are words that also come up a lot.

Hyperactivity, on the other hand, is more clearly defined as restlessness, resulting in excessive activity. Hyperactives are usually described as having "ants in their pants." (ADHD, the first category recognized in medicine some 75 years ago, is a combination of hyperactivity and ADD.)

According to the American Psychiatric Association, a person has ADHD if they meet eight or more of the following paraphrased criteria:

1. They can't remain seated if required to do so.
2. They are easily distracted by extraneous stimuli.

114

3. Focusing on a single task or play activity is difficult.

4. Frequently begin another activity without completing the first.

5. Fidgets or squirms (or feels restless mentally).

6. Can't (or doesn't want to) wait for his turn during group activities.

7. Will often interrupt with an answer before a question is completed.

8. Has problems with chore or job follow-through.

9. Can't play quietly easily.

10. Impulsively jumps into physically dangerous activities without weighing the consequences.

11. Easily loses things (pencils, tools, papers) necessary to complete school or work projects.

12. Interrupts others inappropriately.

13. Talks impulsively or excessively.

14. Doesn't seem to listen when spoken to.

Three caveats to keep in mind: The behaviors must have started before age seven, not represent some other form of classifiable mental illness and occur more frequently than the average person of the same age.

Characteristics of people with ADD

Let's look at the characteristics generally ascribed to people with ADD in more detail:

Easily distracted—Since ADD people are constantly "scoping out" everything around them, focusing on a single item is difficult. Just try having a conversation with an ADD person while a television is on.

Short, but very intense, attention span—Though it can't be defined in terms of minutes or hours, anything an ADD person finds boring immediately loses their attention. Other projects may hold their rapt and extraordinarily intense attention for hours or days.

Disorganization—ADD children and adults are often chronically disorganized—their rooms are messy, their desk a shambles, their files incoherent. While people without ADD can certainly be equally messy and disorganized, they can usually find what they are looking for; ADDers *can't*.

Distortions of time-sense—ADDers have an exaggerated sense of urgency when they're working on something and an exaggerated sense of boredom when they have nothing interesting to do.

Difficulty following directions—A new theory on this aspect holds that ADDers have difficulty processing auditory or verbal information. A significant aspect of this difficulty is the very-common reports of parents of ADD kids who say their kids love to watch TV and hate to read.

Daydream—Or fall into depressions or mood-swings.

Take risks—ADDers seem to make faster decisions than non-ADDers. Which is why Thom Hartmann and Wilson Harrell, former publisher of *Inc.* magazine and author of ***For Entrepreneurs Only***, conclude that the vast majority of successful entrepreneurs probably have ADD! They call them "Hunters", as opposed to the more staid "Farmer" types.

Easily frustrated and impatient—ADDers do *not* beat around the bush or suffer fools gladly. They are direct and to-the-point. When things aren't working, "Do something!" is the ADD rallying cry, even if that something is a bad idea.

Why ADD kids have trouble in school

First and foremost, says Thom Hartmann, it's because schools are set up for "Farmers"—sit at a desk, do what you're told, watch and listen to the teacher. This is pure hell for the "Hunters" with ADD. The bigger the class size, the worse it becomes. Kids with ADD, remember, are easily distracted, easily bored, easily turned off, always ready to move on.

What should you look for in a school setting to make it more palatable to an ADD son or daughter? What can you do at home to help your child (or yourself)? Hartmann has some solid answers:

- ***Learning needs to be project- and experience-based***, providing more opportunities for creativity and shorter and smaller "bites" of information. Many "gifted" programs offer exactly such opportunities. The problem for many kids with ADD is that they've spent years in non-gifted, Farmer-type classroom settings and may be labeled underachieving behavior problems, effectively shut out of the programs virtually designed for them! Many parents report that children diagnosed as ADD, who failed miserably in public school, thrived in private school. Hartmann attributes this to the smaller classrooms, more individual attention with specific goal-setting, project-based learning and similar methods common in such schools. These factors are just what make ADD kids thrive!

- *Create a weekly performance template* on which *both* teacher and parent chart the child's performance, positive and negative. "Creating such a larger-than-the-child system," claims Hartmann, "will help keep ADD children on task and on time.

- *Encourage special projects for extra credit.* Projects give ADDers the chance to learn in the mode that's most appropriate to them. They will also give such kids the chance to make up for the "boring" homework they sometimes simply can't make themselves do.

- *Stop labeling them "disordered."* Kids react to labels, especially negative ones, even more than adults. Saying "you have a deficit and a disorder" may be more destructive than useful.

- *Think twice about medication,* but don't discard it as an option. Hartmann has a very real concern about the long-term side effects of the drugs normally prescribed for ADDers. He also notes that they may well be more at risk to be substance abusers as adults, so starting them on medication at a young age sends a very mixed message. On the other hand, if an ADD child cannot have his or her special needs met in the classroom, *not* medicating him or her may be a disaster. "The relatively unknown long-term risks of drug therapy," says Hartmann, "may be more than offset by the short-term benefits of improved classroom performance."

Specific suggestions about time management

- *Use all the time-management forms in this book*, without fail, every single day. Reprioritize, replan, reschedule as needed—and that will probably be more often than others without ADD. And *don't look too far ahead*—concentrate your efforts on short-term goals.

- *Organize your time around tasks*. ADDers do well with short bursts of high-quality effort and attention. So *every* task—personal, educational, social or professional—should be broken into the smallest possible "bite-size" chunks. While this will make an ADDer's calendar, to do list or priority task sheet appear incredibly long and crowded, the smaller the tasks, the more will be accomplished.

- *Break everything into specific goal units*. ADDers are very goal-oriented; as soon as they reach one, it's on to the next. So establishing *very* short-term goals is essential. Make goals specific, definable and measurable. And stick to only one priority at a time.

- *Create distraction-free zones.* Henry David Thoreau (who evidently suffered from ADD, by the way) was so desperate to escape distraction he moved to isolated Walden Pond. Organize your time and workspace to create your own "Walden Pond", especially when you have to write, take notes, read or study. ADDers need silence, so consider the library. Another tip: Clean your work area thoroughly at the end of each day. This will minimize distractions as you try to write.

Manage Your Time

- *Train your attention span.* ADDers will probably never be able to train themselves to ignore distractions totally, but a variety of meditation techniques might help them stay focused longer.

- *Utilize short-term rewards.* ADD salespeople don't do well when a sales contest lasts for six months, even if the reward is spectacular, like a 10-day cruise. But stick a $100 bill on the wall and watch them focus! Those with ADD will not be motivated by rewards that are too ephemeral or too far in the future. They live for the here and now and need to be rewarded immediately.

Chapter Nine

TIME MANAGEMENT FORMS

In this chapter, I've included blank copies of each of the three key tools introduced in this book: the Priority Task Sheet, Daily Schedule and Term Planning Calendar forms. Please photocopy as many of these forms as you need, enlarge them to fit in your notebook, and adapt them in any way you see fit to *use* them in *your* time management program.

Happy planning. And congratulations on committing to a successful time management program!

Manage Your Time

Term Planning Calendar

Fill in due dates for assignments and papers, dates of tests, and important non-academic activities and events

Month	Mon	Tue	Wed	Thu	Fri	Sat	Sun

Priority Rating	Scheduled?	**Priority Tasks This Week** *Week of* ▨ *through* ▨

Manage Your Time

Daily Schedule

date:

Assignments Due	Schedule	
	5	
	6	
	7	
	8	
	9	
To Do/Errands	10	
	11	
	12	
	1	
	2	
	3	
	4	
	5	
Homework	6	
	7	
	8	
	9	
	10	
	11	
	12	

Time

INDEX

Manage Your Time